WHAT PEOPLE ARE SAYING ABOUT

WHY RELIGIONS WORK

A refreshing and timely perspective on the spiritual condition of our times, reminding us that the basic role of religion is the cure of souls and calling for a renewed respect for religious traditions and an acknowledgement of the vital part they play in the maintenance of human community – contrary to the strident assertions of outspoken militant atheists. Radhakrishnan's vision of a religion of the spirit, endorsed by Pope Benedict XVI, gives us an inspiring prospect of unity within diversity.

David Lorimer, Programme Director of the international Scientific and Medical Network, editor with Oliver Robinson of *A New Renaissance: Transforming Science, Spirit and Society.*

In her new book Dr. Eleanor Stoneham, who is herself a trained empirical scientist, presents the rational evidence to demonstrate that the genuine religious quest has just as good a claim as the scientific method to be a search for truth. Her open-mindedness is in contrast to the intolerance purveyed in many New Atheist publications where religious people are stereotyped as too stupid or ill informed to take account of the findings of modern science. Such a wild generalization is itself unintelligent because it is manifestly untrue, as Dr. Stoneham demonstrates. She argues that open-minded compassion lies at the heart of all true religion. Its absence is a sure sign of betrayal, leading to every sort of corruption. The New Atheists should be aware that they do their cause no good by showing a similar closed-minded lack of respect.

David Hay, Honorary Senior Research Fellow, Department of Divinity & Religious Studies King's College Aberdeen Uni~~~ and author with Rebecca Nye of *The Spirit*

We are smashing up our relationships, our planet and ourselves. Religion is often blamed, and the charges often seem just. Fundamentalism of all sorts puts words and dogmas above people, justice and plain decency.

There's a strong temptation to ditch religion. Compassionate humanism sometimes seems to have a more sensitive diagnostic nose and a more shrewd therapeutic, or at least palliative, plan. But ditching religion, argues Eleanor Stoneham in this gentle, urgent, compelling book, would be a bad mistake. It would mean reading religion as its twisters – the strident Christian Taliban of the Bible Belt and the dead-eyed, red-handed Islamists – want us to read it. We would be joining them in their crass misreading.

The real core of religion, she contends, is the Golden Rule of passionate altruism – a rule shared by all the great world faiths and by all great-hearted people. This rule wasn't generated by the Darwinian imperatives of reciprocal altruism or kin selection: it was set into the hearts of men by a God who gives himself freely and wildly to his creatures. We cannot do without him (or her), as Stoneham calmly and persuasively demonstrates, and it's dangerous and downright dull to try.

Charles Foster, Fellow of Green Templeton College, University of Oxford, author of *Wired for God? The Biology of Spiritual Experience.*

Why Religions Work

God's Place in the World Today

Why Religions Work

God's Place in the World Today

Eleanor Stoneham

Winchester, UK
Washington, USA

First published by Circle Books, 2012
Circle Books is an imprint of John Hunt Publishing Ltd., Laurel House, Station Approach,
Alresford, Hants, SO24 9JH, UK
office1@jhpbooks.net
www.johnhuntpublishing.com
www.circle-books.com

For distributor details and how to order please visit the 'Ordering' section on our website.

Text copyright: Eleanor Stoneham 2012

ISBN: 978 1 78099 496 3

A CIP catalogue record for this book is available from the British Library.

Design: Stuart Davies

Printed in the USA by Edwards Brothers Malloy

We operate a distinctive and ethical publishing philosophy in all
areas of our business, from our global network of authors to
production and worldwide distribution.

CONTENTS

From the arrogance that thinks it knows all truth,
From the cowardice that shrinks from new truth,
From the laziness that is content with half-truths,
O God of truth, deliver us.

Anon

Acknowledgements

I am grateful to many people who have supported and helped me in various ways while writing this book.

My friends as ever are a source of strength and refreshment when the going has been tough. Often I have found it necessary to take time out away from the distractions of home and garden and I am thankful to my long-suffering family and for those friends and colleagues who have willingly stood in for my church duties at such times.

Then there are those who have most kindly and generously found time in their own busy schedules to read the script in whole or in part and made valuable suggestions. In particular I thank Dr Edi Bilimoria, Yvonne Louis, Dr Adam Stoneham and Hannah McSorley. The book is all the better for their input, although of course I take full responsibility for any faults and errors that remain, which are mine alone.

Finally I am grateful to John Hunt Publishing, and also to David Lorimer, Dr David Hay and Charles Foster for their encouragement and for endorsing my work.

I thank them all.

Eleanor Stoneham
April 2012
www.eleanorstoneham.com
eleanorstoneham@hotmail.com

Introduction

There is only one religion, though there are a hundred versions of it.
George Bernard Shaw

Sebaki Tandi was just seven months old when her mother died. She was sent to her uncle and at an early age started to work as a servant girl in neighbors' homes. This happens to many youngsters in India, especially girls from poor Christian backgrounds, and they miss out on any education, becoming destined to a life of menial labor. The Church of North India has set up hostels to provide children like Sebaki with an education, with support from USPG: Anglicans in World Mission. Sebaki went to such a hostel when she was 10 and her life was turned around.[1]

The Tanzanian island of Misali on the East African coast is an important nesting site for turtles and has wonderful corals reefs that support the fish population.[2] Local fishermen were destroying this ecosystem by the indiscriminate use of dynamite to literally blow the fish out of the water. This made their fishing easier, the catch more certain. But of course this was killing young fish alongside those of an edible size, as well as destroying the coral habitat on which the fish population depends. Carrying on like this, the livelihood of the fishing community would soon be destroyed for good. Attempts to educate the fishermen through leaflets had no effect, and neither did imposing a ban on this method of fishing. The law was simply flouted. Scientists even suggested the somewhat desperate measure of armed patrols to apprehend the culprits. All this was to no avail. But by appealing to the Muslim faith of the fishermen, through the community sheik leaders, the fishermen were persuaded that what they were doing was wrong, that dynamite fishing is illegal according to the laws of Islam. For the Qur'an teaches "O children of Adam!... eat and drink: but waste not by excess for Allah loveth not the wasters."[3]

These are two stories from very different parts of the world. But both have a happy ending, thanks to religion.

It is fashionable to knock God.

Books that do tend to become bestsellers.

But much of the atheist anger seems to be directed at some of the worst aspects of organized religion. It is accompanied by what appear to be serious calls for the abolition of all religions, as if that were at all possible, let alone wise.

I don't believe that the success of the atheist literature is all about ditching God. I think it has much more to do with touching nerves; it speaks to a widely felt disenchantment with what some organized religion has offered in the recent past, alongside a feeling that religion is not relevant and meaningful in the 21st century. This becomes further fuelled by a deep-seated historical religious prejudice for past wrongs and by widely held misperceptions of what religion offers today.

The main role of the religions should be to look after our spiritual life. We sometimes rather quaintly call this the 'cure' of souls. We are spiritual beings. So alongside the drift away from religion and the general decline in congregations in both America and Europe over the last few decades[4] we have also seen an increasing interest in spirituality, in its broadest sense. Without religion people soon find that there is something missing in their lives, some hard-to-describe quality that may be called Spirit, the Other, Presence, even God. Indeed many, myself included, are calling for the need to enhance and nurture spiritual literacy if we are to build a better world for all.[5]

Recent surveys show that 83% of Americans identify with a religious denomination, mostly as Protestant, Protestant Episcopal or Catholic Christians, and 40% state that they attend services nearly every week or more.[6] In the UK the numbers are somewhat lower, but despite what the media would have us believe, the Christian faith still claims 58% of the UK adult population, and 15% of UK adults still go to church at least once a month.[7] Bucking the trend of a general slow decline in religious observance in the West, UK Cathedral attendance figures are in fact climbing. The fact is that across the world, organized religion is still a huge element in most people's lives. Depending on how the figures are compiled, somewhere between 66% and 90% of the world population have a religion or faith. This is a force to be reckoned with and it is not to be dismissed out of hand on the basis of a passing fashion. What is more these numbers are not declining, since the increases in population are happening in those countries where faith is strongest.[8]

Organized religion is very much still with us. It shows no real signs of going away!

Perhaps this is why the popular atheists such as Daniel Dennett, Sam Harris, Richard Dawkins, the late Christopher Hitchens and others become more strident in their abuse of religion. They feel under attack, threatened by indisputable statistics about the strength of religions in the world. Their cries that religion is done are a load of smokes and mirrors. The real picture is very different.

If something is not going to go away, isn't it better to find ways to work with it, rather than against it? It is true that religions also need to change. They need to find ways to become more relevant for the lives we now lead and to help us live those lives true to our faith and the ancient and spiritual values of the sacred texts. But healing our world depends now more than ever on supporting the faith groups, not knocking them.

In the following chapters I explain why.

What do the best-selling atheists of our time want anyway and why are they wrong? I assume that they must want a better world. They seek the abolition of religions because they blame religions for war, violence and grief. Only by abolishing faith will violence and war be eliminated, they say.[9] But there are other, richer, less simplistic, more humane ways to look at the picture.

Chief Rabbi Jonathan Sacks once wrote that excuses abound for war and violence without any need for religion. I shall look at the question of wars and also some of the other flawed assumptions that tar the image of religion.

So this book is also a rebuke to militant atheism.

There are books that reply to the angry atheists by tackling theology and philosophy and explaining why there is a God. I want to defend religion simply for what it is and what it can and does offer the world. As the opening stories show, religions offer far more than spiritual care; they are the largest and most important source of social capital that we have. So do we need religions? I hope to show you not only why the answer is a resounding and definite 'Yes' but also what is needed to bring them back to their rightful place in society. I want to dispel many misconceptions about them. Even if you do not believe in God, there is still an urgent need to support the concept and reality of religion, to stop knocking it and to stop knocking God.

Of course there are differences between the faiths; sometimes they seem irreconcilable. Religious leaders do not always help their own cause, while in fact a huge amount of time and energy is being spent by faith groups in working together on common and often linked global problems, such as the relief of poverty, hunger, disease and other social injustices, dealing with violence, a decline in moral values, climate change issues and so on. Yet the media focus is on differences of detail in dogma, debates on gender issues, recriminations about past and indeed present wrongs, and historical violence. We need to redress the balance in the ways religions are portrayed by the media: to look for the positive. We need to be wary of the certainty of the angry atheists. Great minds *don't* think alike and fools seldom differ. One does not need God to be a bigot.

But is tolerance the right answer? Tolerance is to do with

'putting up with' something. It is not the opposite of intolerance; the one fuels the other, as simmering tolerance implies condescension, superiority and prejudice, and lies in wait to erupt into violence given the right conditions, rather as the smoldering bonfire will suddenly spring to life if a breeze blows up to fan the flames. So we need much more than mere tolerance. But what is the alternative?

The interface between religion and spirituality is at best unclear, often controversial and the subject of much academic debate. Do religion and spirituality go hand in hand? Can we have one without the other? Which came first? Is one an identifiable aspect of the other? Do they need each other? None of these questions are easy to answer. But while the literature on spirituality is immense, the subject in all its variants of understanding simply vast, it is very relevant here and I shall explain why.

I am a Christian. This may be reflected from time to time in what I write, although some may find my views unconventional, perhaps even heretical. I am also a trained research scientist. I hope this book will help laity and clergy alike relate church tradition to the wider world of science, spirituality and interfaith issues. This book is also aimed at the 'spiritual but not religious', and those convinced that their own particular religion or faith is the only way to enlightenment, the only path to Truth.

I want to show you all why religion, and this includes the finer aspects of organized religion, has a vital role to play in shaping the world towards a better future for us all; why religions cannot be ignored, should not be abused; and yes, how they also need to change.

I want to approach the God and religion argument from a new angle.

Of one thing I am sure. There is simply not enough respect for religions, particularly in the Western world. I want this book to be a serious yet accessible contribution to understanding why we all need to support religion as well as spirituality. Further, I want to explore how a global spiritual awareness, an appreciation of spiritual human interconnectivity and shared responsibilities will help. Are ideas of spirituality and advances in the scientific understanding of empathy and consciousness closing the gap between science and religion, between spirituality and religion? Could these same ideas help us find better inter-religious and interdenominational understanding? Perhaps so. Such questions matter for the future of our world. We need spirituality. And we need religion.[10] We need them both very much indeed.

We alone among living creatures have hindsight, foresight and freedom of choice. The world population has hit 7 billion, and there may be 9 billion of us by 2050. We are now steering our own evolution. Never mind Charles Darwin, who is quite wrongly accused of abolishing God with his theories on evolution.[11] Life as we know it on this planet is changing inexorably and often dangerously, at our own hands.

Pierre Teilhard de Chardin back in 1978 wrote:

… unless adult Humanity is to drift aimlessly and so to perish, it is essential that it rise to the concept of a specifically and integrally *human effort*. After having for so long done no more than allow itself to live, Humanity will one day understand that the time has come to undertake its own development and to mark out its own road.[12]

For this to happen we need a big change in attitude. We need to change the way we think about religions.

Chapter 1

Why Religions Work: Social Capital Writ Large!

From now on, the great religions of the world will no longer declare war on each other, but on the giants that afflict [humankind].
Charles Bonney, 1893 Parliament of the World's Religions.

Etelvina and her husband live in rural Guatemala with their twin seven-year-old boys. Making a living is not easy there. For years, Etelvina was forced to travel around the country looking for work opportunities, with no luck. But then the Episcopal Diocese of Guatemala, in partnership with Episcopal Relief & Development, gave her a micro-finance loan to help her buy ingredients and equipment to start her own business selling tortillas, and to help her husband buy more vegetable seeds for the garden. The extra money they can now make between them is improving their living conditions and helping them to give their children an education.[13]

There are huge inequalities across the world in terms of standards of living, availability of food, water, adequate and safe shelter, proper sanitation, education and health welfare, and the ability to work gainfully; all of these are basic human rights.

And wherever in the world help is needed, the world's religions are there, providing food and shelter, helping with finance to support business opportunities, fighting disease and promoting health, responding rapidly to humanitarian disasters both natural and man-made, and most importantly also helping people get back on their feet again, build their independence.

Every year organizations such as Episcopal Relief and Development and CAFOD, the Catholic aid agency, along with many others, reach out to millions of people in many different countries to provide essential aid; bringing hope, compassion and solidarity to poor communities, standing side by side with them to end poverty and injustice; helping to create a safer, more sustainable and peaceful world. There are dozens if not hundreds of such organizations; as well as those just mentioned, the USPG Anglicans in World Mission, Christian Aid, Islamic Relief Worldwide, Jewish Care, Muslim Aid and the Salvation Army are just a few of the better known ones but there are many others.

All this valuable work is born out of the compassion for our fellow beings that is taught in all religious traditions.

The world's great religions are social capital writ large! Why? Because they have a huge advantage over governments. They are able to take a long-term view. It is a well-known adage that the Vatican thinks in terms of centuries. Religions can do the same. They are also sometimes one of the few local institutions that people will trust and turn to for help. And they all have enviable and well-established global networks, reaching into the most remote areas of the world, along with deep resources, that when combined can be potent catalysts for change.

The way that religious networks help relieve suffering and fight injustices across the world should be of concern to us all, if for no other reason than that injustices fuel unrest, and unrest can escalate into violence and worse. But equally important must be the humanitarian issue. Extreme weather conditions in poorer parts of the world have enormous potential implications in terms of human misery and mass migrations of people. Where will all these displaced people go? And surely we must all be able to feel something of the misery and pain suffered by so many, brought very much alive to us on our television screens; even if we try to push these images to the back of our minds most of the time.

Those of us who are fortunate enough to live in the affluent Western world are steeped in our materialist culture that is in fact dominating the whole world. Other less well 'developed' countries see our gizmos and gadgets and styles of living and envy us. Who can blame them? They want to pile in and share the perceived 'riches' of our way of life, have the 'stuff' that we burden our lives with. But in our hearts we have a sense that the modern high-speed technological materialistic lifestyle that so many of us have bought into is not doing us any good. We are losing relationship, connection, with other humans and with nature. Even shopping can now be done entirely with no human contact, just a machine that tells us when to put our card in the slot and accuses us that we have put an unusual item in the bagging area, a euphemism that this machine thinks we are trying to steal something! Much of our individual wealth, such as we may have, tends to be then soaked up by ever-bigger energy guzzling houses, and more technology, with negative ecological and sociological effects.

The point is that this Western way of life is damaging the planet and its wildlife. This has been the most dominant environmental concern for the last 20 years. Natural habitats are becoming degraded; we are seeing a loss of biodiversity, alongside water pollution and the emission of climate changing gases. But shortages of natural resources are likely to bite before the worst climate change effects. Shortages of energy, water and food, for example, will be reflected in costly price inflation, that will hurt first those of us in the developed West who have the most 'stuff' and the highest standards of living. It already takes Earth something like eighteen months to replenish the resources we use globally in a year. If everyone shared our levels of consumption in the West, we would need somewhere between three to five planets like Earth to sustain us. Common sense tells us that the figures simply do not add up. Americans have the highest ecological footprint in the world, about twice that of Europeans. Both are too big to be sustainable in the long-term.[14]

Whatever our individual views on the reality and causes of global warming and climate change, we can all see the violent natural disasters for ourselves, and observe that the poorest among us suffer the most for the damage caused when houses collapse or are washed or blown away, livestock drowns or starves to death, disease spreads through stricken areas. There is now widespread scientific agreement on the parlous state of the environment, in spite of the cynics and skeptics who like to believe that it is all fake, who would love to believe that the earth will always be able to sustain the profligate Western lifestyle as it spreads across the whole world. Earth has finite resources and is groaning. We should have no illusions as to the urgent action now required.

This is where the world's religions again play a vitally important role.

Those same well-established global networks that can so effectively provide relief and support for the world's disadvantaged people are also responsible for significant environmental initiatives. Such work is of course a question of faith in action, since Christians, Muslims, Hindus, Buddhists, Daoists, Jews and most if not all the world's other religions share a common belief in the need to respect and care for creation and the natural world, a belief that it is morally wrong to damage the environment. The problem is that we often simply choose to ignore this as we go about our daily lives.

At the end of a rutted dirt road near the small town of Ripton in Addison County, Vermont, on the western slopes of the Green Mountains, a labyrinth of footpaths weaves between the trees and alongside the streams within peaceful and unspoiled woodland. Each path is dedicated to one of the world's religions or spiritualities, and has texts along the way to help the walker connect between the sacred and the natural world. The mission of these Spirit in Nature Interfaith Paths[15] is to provide "a place of interconnecting paths where people of diverse spiritual traditions may walk, worship, meet, meditate, and promote education and action toward better stewardship of this sacred earth." There is a sacred circle where the paths all meet, emphasizing the interconnections between the different religions, and between man and his environment. This project is just one of many described on the site of the Forum on Religion and Ecology at Yale,[16] one of the largest international multi-religious projects of its kind. The Forum exists to broaden the understanding of the many complex issues involved in today's environmental concerns, and all this within a religious and multidisciplinary context that Yale is so well placed to provide.

The ancient settlement of Luss sits on the beautiful banks of Loch Lomond within Scotland's first national park, the Trossachs. Luss has been a place of Christian pilgrimage for 1,500 years. St Kessog preached here and died at the hands of Druids in the year 510. Luss has become part of the Green Pilgrimage Network,[17] a major new global initiative launched in Assisi in November 2011 that is addressing the huge environmental impact of the many pilgrimages to various sacred sites and holy cities across the world, involving millions of pilgrim journeys each year. As part of the same project a Green Hajj Guide has been produced, aimed at the two million Muslim pilgrims who visit Mecca in Saudi Arabia each year for the Hajj, the biggest annual pilgrimage in the world.

The Green Pilgrimage Network is just one of the many positive religious projects that have been launched and are supported by the Alliance of Religions and Conservation (ARC). This is a secular organization, founded back in 1995 by Prince Philip, Duke of Edinburgh. The ARC has a vision "of people, through their beliefs, treading more gently upon the earth," and a twofold strategy "to help faiths realize their potential to be proactive on environmental issues and to help secular groups recognize this and become active partners." The real catalyst for change came when each religion or faith involved in the initial discussions was asked to prepare a statement explaining their place in the context of creation and ecology. An initial meeting developed into a worldwide network of faith groups working on ecological and development issues, and by the time the ARC was formally launched at Windsor Castle in 1995 there were nine religions involved and thousands of environmental projects in hand, initiating much extremely valuable and far reaching conservation work.

I have written about the ARC at greater length elsewhere so will not dwell on it here.[18] But what it stands for is worth repeating simply because of the substantial work the religions are all doing, often in collaboration or cooperation with others, towards ensuring the earth's future protection through the work of umbrella organizations such as the ARC and the Yale Forum on Religion and Ecology. What wonderful opportunities such organizations provide for building bridges of understanding, cooperation and respect between religions of many different faiths and creeds.

And there are many other good stories to tell.

One problem we seem to have is that so many of us, while accepting the need for sustainable living, feel that anything we can do is hopeless in the face of the much publicized industrial expansion in China and the rapid proliferation of coal fired power stations there. But the Chinese Government is listening to the concerns of the world and turning to religion, to its own Daoist followers,[19] for their wisdom and advice on environmental matters. "No one disputes the astonishing growth of consumerism and wealth in China today and increasingly China is trying to address whether this is sustainable," said Martin Palmer, Secretary General of the Alliance of Religions and Conservation. "But maybe deeper than this," he continues, "is the question of whether China can also be compassionate, wise and community-focused once again. This is why the Chinese Communist government for the first time ever is meeting with the Daoists of China (China's oldest religion) to see how this ancient wisdom and spirituality might put a heart back into the ever-expanding body of modern China."

There are many religious organizations across the globe working towards a more environmentally friendly way of living for us all: The Episcopal Ecological Network, Earth Quaker Action Team, the multi-faith Australian Religious Response to Climate Change, the European Christian Environmental Network and many more.[20]

In 2007 the UK Environment Agency asked leading scientists and environmentalists, for their ideas on the 50 most important things that will save the planet. High up on the list at number two was the vital role that religious and faith leaders can collectively play. "Organized religion of all denominations, PLEASE get your congregations to make caring for our rapidly decomposing, landfill site of a planet the utmost priority," pleaded one respondent. "They need to form a coalition to encourage their followers to set an example to the rest of the population," said another.[21]

In fact, scarcely noticed by many secular environmentalists, the combined religious and faith groups have been the fastest growing environmental movement globally. It is true that the initial awakening of faith leaders to environmental and sustainability awareness took time. Now few are unaware of the issues involved, or are not involved in some way in leading action.[22]

The world's religions also have an enormous influence in education; indeed they are involved in the running and support of more than 50% of the world's schools. Through such schools, and also via various relief and aid organizations, religions play an essential role in tackling female illiteracy and population issues, and in providing health education and services, often concentrating on education for poor underprivileged children. Religions may provide the only hope of education in the poorest parts of the world. In the developed West such schools also have a history of providing better educational performance than their non-faith counterparts. Where faith or parochial schools are available in an area, they prove popular among parents for the values that they teach. A decline of parochial Catholic schools in the States seems to be more to do with demographics than lack of interest. In the UK Church schools are turning children away for lack of space.

The evidence is strong. Are so many parents likely to be far wrong? Or are we dangerously brainwashing impressionable young children? And what is the difference between faith schools and the atheist schools that some would like to see established? That rather depends on how the children are taught of course. It is vitally important to teach them from an early age about the world's different religions, but emphasis should be placed on the many features common to them all, so that these can be appreciated and celebrated while helping the children to understand and respect the smaller number of differences. Of course children need to be made to think for themselves about their faiths. But most important of all is the need to nurture the spirituality within these children so that they grow in spiritual as well as religious literacy. What is wrong with that?

What else do religions offer a hurting world? For a start they demand ethical obligations in the contexts of family and society. They teach love and honesty, self- denial and self-sacrifice and promote living according to need rather than greed.

But is religion needed to support ethics and morality? The humanists would argue that they need no religious code of conduct to tell them that they should behave in a 'decent' fashion. That's all to the well and good, if you are well educated and have been brought up in a family that teaches such values. But let's not forget that the values that we promote for the good of society, values such as love, compassion, honesty and non-violence, have their origins in the teachings of the ancient wisdoms and faiths.

There is a threefold morality that comes from all the great Holy teachers, from Jesus, the Buddha, from the Mosaic laws of the Old Testament, from the Upanishads, and the 8 limbs of

Yoga,[23] for example. They all call for a behavioral code grounded in right conduct in thought and speech and deed. Phiroz Mehta sees this threefold morality as the "foundation for living as an integrated human being," extolling values that distinguish the human from the sub human. If we abide by these rules there will be no inner or outer conflict in living our lives.[24]

Mehta tells the Buddhist Parable of the Saw, where the Buddha teaches his monks how to behave in the face of all the bad things that people can do to them:

> Neither shall our minds be affected by this, nor for this matter shall we give vent to evil words, but we shall remain full of concern and pity, with a mind of love, and we shall not give in to hatred. On the contrary, we shall live projecting thoughts of universal love to that very person, making him as well as the whole world the object of our thoughts of universal love – thoughts that have grown great, exalted and measureless. We shall dwell radiating these thoughts which are void of hostility and ill will.[25]

This simple morality, with nurturing, flowers into virtue, or what Mehta describes as "the transcendental ethic by which the true human lives."

I think a great fallacy within the criticisms of so many vociferous atheists and humanists is that they are fond of portraying religions in the worst light: and such comments are nowhere more adamant than around the question of ethics and morals. The critics are fond of quoting stories of awful deeds done in the name of religion, the Inquisitions and some terrorist attacks, for example. We cannot deny these. But causes are often to be found in religious fanaticism and in civilizations less advanced than our own. Dreadful atrocities were committed in the history of the Western world to robbers and kings alike. And the Western justice systems may not be perfect. But we are at least much more civilized now in our treatment of wrongdoers and we have the benefit of an education not available to many across the world. But a word of warning: Gandhi didn't think much of our Western Civilization either. When asked what he thought of it, he reputedly retorted that "it would be a good idea."

So do we need religions to support moral behavior? In a sense the question does not matter, it is even the wrong question. The Dalai Lama writes: "whether a person is a religious believer does not matter much. Far more important is that they be a good human being."[26] But he has observed that religion and ethics were once closely intertwined and warns that since the influence of religion has declined in so many lives there is "mounting confusion with respect to the problem of how best we are to conduct ourselves in life... morality becomes a matter of individual preference."[27]

Martin Luther King saw this. He observed that "the richer we have become materially the poorer we have become morally and spiritually." We live, he said, in two realms:

The internal is that realm of spiritual ends expressed in art, literature, morals, and religion. The external is that complex of devices, techniques, mechanisms, and instrumentalities by means of which we live. Our problem today is that we have allowed the internal to become lost in the external. We have allowed the means by which we live to outdistance the ends for which we live.

And he further warned that racial injustice, poverty and war would only be alleviated if we balance our moral progress with our scientific progress and learn the practical art of living in harmony in a "worldwide fellowship that lifts neighborly concern beyond one's tribe, race, class, and nation."[28]

To be sure, the great religious texts and teachers lay down codes of behavior that few can argue with, and we can allow these to be our teacher, our guidance and our wisdom regardless of our religious persuasions. So we should be asking ourselves whether we should be teaching the values and virtues of the great religions and religious leaders as a basis for our behavior in this world. The answer for any thinking person to the question put in this way surely has to be a resounding 'yes!' When we look at the immorality in the world, an alternative secular and materialist society does not seem to have served us well.

So we see that religious or faith groups are working tirelessly in many different and positive ways for the good of all humanity. Quite apart from the more obvious and visible relief programs delivering aid to areas of suffering in the world they are quietly working for the benefit of communities at a more local level, helping youth, or the homeless, providing night time support on the streets of our inner cities, providing food, shelter and counseling where needed, making sure youngsters are safe, all in the name of a compassionate and loving God, who teaches that we should "do unto others that which we would have done unto ourselves."

But public awareness of much of this work is limited. Why? It is quite simply that our biased media do so much to emphasize the negative, and play down the positive where religious reporting is concerned. And if the atheists dwell at all on such good works, they are inclined to accuse us of simply striving to gain points towards our future salvation or of putting up "perfumed smokescreens!"[29]

And of course the sheer numbers and scale of strongly held religious beliefs are a force to be reckoned with. Christianity is still the faith to which 78% of North Americans, 58% of the UK, and 33% of the world's population turn for their healing and spiritual nourishment. Taken together Christians and Muslims account for more than 50% of the world's population. Add to those numbers the first of the great Abrahamic Faiths, Judaism, and it has to be clear that religion is not going to go away.

But here is a further important point. When the different faiths work together with a common purpose, for example through cooperative relief agencies such as CAFOD, then we find real and positive opportunities for fostering inter-religious tolerance, respect and understanding.

When we add to this the massive amount of vital social work being done by religions away from the public gaze often at local community level, doesn't it become clearer that we need to work more with religion, not against it?

What would happen to all the many people needing and receiving help across the world if all these organizations, inspired and supported by religion, were to close down their operations? Can the new atheists and humanists seriously want this? I think not.

Now I know that religions can be criticized for not always being true to their teaching. For example during the Occupy Wall Street demonstrations against capitalism and corporate greed that spread around the world in 2011, the Church of England was accused of hypocrisy in their threatened eviction of the Occupy London demonstrators outside St. Paul's Cathedral. Religions do often need to honestly reappraise themselves and make changes as necessary in the light of societal changes.

Of course religions are not perfect, nor free from criticism. How could they be, organized and run as they are by fallible human beings? But they offer so much to the world; our societies depend on the tireless work of the many different religious charities, often supplied through unpaid volunteers.

Whatever the differences between us relating to spirituality, religion and faith, we simply do not have time to iron them all out. We need to put them to one side and curb our bickering. Instead we should be celebrating what we have in common, understanding and respecting our differences, and seeking ways to work together as human beings, with all our individual frailties, for the mutual benefit of the one beautiful and finite planet earth we all have to share.

We have a fine inheritance in our many different faiths, religions, spiritualities and ancient philosophies. They are a part of life's rich pattern, providing a splendid tapestry of experience, wisdom and sacred texts, with so many common features to celebrate and differences to learn from. It is time to look at some of these.

Chapter 2

Our Rich Faith Inheritance and Our Shared Values

As far as I know, God is not sectarian. He is not obsessed with minor details of doctrine. We should quickly liberate ourselves from theological conflict which results from blind attachment to doctrines and rituals, and instead focus on living communication with God.
Andrew Wilson, World Scripture[30]

The world's great religions display a wonderfully varied and rich tapestry of different beliefs. Equally they are all united in so many ways, in similar teachings and shared values. In particular they all share much the same mission when it comes to loving one another and healing our planet. And all of this is undergirded by their ancient wisdoms and sacred texts.

The Sacred Scriptures

World Scripture: A Comparative Anthology of Sacred Texts[31] is an extraordinary reference work. It brings together in one volume over 4000 passages, from 268 Sacred texts and 55 oral traditions, gathered comparatively around 165 topics. In its 928 pages this book compares passages from the sacred writings of all the world's great religions on all the significant issues of the religious life; our universal concerns about salvation, sin, faith, prayer, self denial, purpose of life, and so on. It's an amazing reference book, a holistic approach to understanding the world's religions, requiring the cooperative labors of more than 40 scholars and religious leaders from every faith over a period of five years.

In a paper[32] delivered by its editor Andrew Wilson to the inaugural assembly of the Inter Religious Federation for World

Peace (IRFWP), in 1991, he said he hoped that this book would become a textbook in religious education for teaching the young how to live together as one global family, how to overcome barriers between religions, races and cultures.

This book admirably demonstrates the very many shared values and universal foundation behind all religions, surely of far greater significance than the differences that are so often used to divide us.

Wilson points out from detailed analysis that all the religions broadly concur on about 80% of the 165 topics covered. Instead of insisting on a religion's uniqueness on the basis of the 20% where it differs, let's celebrate the common ground on that shared 80%, Wilson urges. What an important tool for promoting world peace this could be, in its emphasis of religious convergence and the universal spiritual truth at the heart of all religion.

Is it being used anywhere in the world for this purpose I wonder? I fear its importance is scarcely recognized.

So what important beliefs do our different religions share?

Love and the Golden Rule

Martin Luther King's friendship with Thich Nhat Hanh inspired him to speak up about the Vietnam War. Both held a firm commitment to non-violence. In his famous speech, *Beyond Vietnam: A Time to Break Silence*, preached at Riverside Church in 1967, King called to place love of neighbor above tribe, race and nation:

When I speak of love... I am speaking of that force which all of the great religions have seen as the supreme unifying principle of life. Love is somehow the key that unlocks the door which leads to ultimate reality... this Hindu-Muslim-Christian-Jewish-Buddhist belief about ultimate... ultimate reality is beautifully summed up in the first epistle of Saint John: "Let us love one another, for love is God. And every one that loveth is born of God and knoweth God. He that loveth not knoweth not God, for God is love." (1 John 4:7–8, 12). "If we love one another, God dwelleth in us and his love is perfected in us."[33]

Of course the principle of loving one another, and furthermore loving our neighbor as ourselves, is embodied in what is called the Golden Rule, and is common to all the world's greatest religions in varying forms.[34]

Confucius probably founded this Golden Rule, in a period of the world's history similar to our own, when societies were being torn apart. It was emphasized 500 years later in the life and teachings of Jesus Christ.

It is around this rule that Karen Armstrong has founded her Charter for Compassion, which I shall revisit in a later chapter in the context of building bridges between faiths. The fact is that we have imperiled ourselves by losing sight of this Golden Rule.

We are all created in the same image

You don't need to believe in God to be able to reflect that we're all basically the same. You only have to look around you with an open mind and with compassion and understanding. Whatever our class, color, race or creed, we're all born and die, suffer physical and mental wounds, have the same basic human needs. We are all of equal worth and value. We have a basic humanity in common.

This is also an important belief across all religions, and vital to remember in later discussions around religious tolerance. For those who believe in God, there is religious authority that we are all the same, in that Genesis tells us that we are all created by the same God and made in God's image. And yet we so often seem to lose sight of this fact, largely through ignorance that fuels fear that can fuel intolerance and worse. It is so important to overcome ignorance. That is why I devote a whole chapter to education later on.

"Every person born into the world represents something new, something that never existed before, something original and unique... If there had been someone like her in the world, there would have been no need for her to be born" (Martin Buber).[35]

Thou shalt not kill

The Golden Rule, based as it is on love, and compassion, and taught by all the great religions, has to be totally incompatible with hurting let alone killing our fellow human beings. The Sixth Commandment of the Old Testament books of Exodus and Deuteronomy is after all "Thou shalt not kill."[36] And many sacred texts go much further, for example:[37]

One should not injure, subjugate, enslave, torture, or kill any animal, living being, organism, or sentient being. This doctrine of nonviolence is immaculate, immutable, and eternal. Just as suffering is painful to you, in the same way it is painful, disquieting, and terrifying to all animals, living beings, organisms, and sentient beings.

Jainism. Acarangasutra 4.25–26

One going to take a pointed stick to pinch a baby bird should first try it on himself to feel how it hurts.

African Traditional Religions. Yoruba Proverb (Nigeria.)

How do you feel when you cause hurt or pain, directly or indirectly, to another sentient being? We could all ask ourselves this question. Do we care? Are we true to our faith or belief structure in everything we do or even remotely cause to happen by our own inactions or actions? Anyone, religious or not, is wide open to criticism by others if their behavior does not reflect their beliefs and values in all ways. This is why I became a vegetarian many years ago.

Faiths and Creation[38]

All the world's faiths share a concern for Creation. Whether or not we believe that our world is God's Creation, we should still be concerned with the beliefs of the main faiths regarding our relationship with the environment. As I have said in the previous chapter, the opportunities for the faiths to work together towards a common purpose are nowhere quite so obvious, and nowhere quite so potent for building inter-religious harmony.[39]

So what do the different religions teach about our relationship with the natural world?

Judaism teaches that it is wrong to over exploit the earth's resources, or behave in such a way as to destroy any species, since all have been created for some purpose. Jews understand the vital importance of preserving the natural balance of Creation. They believe that the entire universe is the work of the Creator, and therefore to love God must mean to love everything He has created, including the inanimate, plants, animals and man. This core belief is behind the Jewish attitude to environmental issues.

At the Islamic Foundation for Ecology and Environmental Science (IFEES)[40] they focus on four Qur'anic principles. The first, unity, is the principle that the human community is part of, as one, with the whole universe. The second, or fitra, says that man's origin is in Creation, and to tamper with it will have repercussions, as indeed we now see all around us. The third principle is that Creation is in balance and that if there is interference with that balance the system simply will not work. And finally, there is responsibility for the earth, which has been left in trust to us as stewards.[41]

The Sikh believes that "a concern for the environment is part of an integrated approach to life and nature. As all Creation has the same origin and end, humans must have consciousness of their place in Creation and their relationship with the rest of Creation. Humans should conduct themselves through life with love, compassion, and justice. Becoming one and being in harmony with God implies that humans endeavor to live in harmony with all of God's Creation."[42]

"Conserve ecology or perish," says the *Bhagavad Gita* (or Song of God), the Hindu sacred scripture. "God's Creation is sacred. Humanity does not have the right to destroy what it cannot create. Humans have to realize the interconnectedness of living entities and emphasize the idea of moral responsibility to oneself, one's society, and the world as a whole." Hindus teach that we can learn spiritual happiness and find fulfillment by living simply and without chasing after material wants and pleasures:

> They have to milk a cow and enjoy, not cut at the udder of the cow with greed to enjoy what is not available in the natural course. Do not use anything belonging to nature, such as oil, coal, or forest, at a greater rate than you can replenish it… do not destroy birds, fish, earthworms, and even bacteria which play vital ecological roles; once they are annihilated you cannot recreate them. Thus only can you avoid becoming bankrupt, and the life cycle can continue for a long, long time.[43]

Doesn't this all make a great deal of sense?

Of all the great faiths and philosophies, the Buddhist seems to understand most clearly not only our need to live more simply and altruistically within the natural world but also the healing power of nature. The Vietnamese monk Venerable Thich Nhat Hanh writes:

> Buddhists believe that the reality of the interconnectedness of human beings, society and Nature will reveal itself more… as we gradually cease to be possessed by anxiety, fear, and the dispersion of the mind. Among the three – human beings,

society and Nature – it is us who begin to effect change. But in order to effect change we must recover ourselves, one must be whole. Since this requires the kind of environment favourable to one's healing, one must seek the kind of lifestyle that is free from the destruction of one's humanness. Efforts to change the environment and to change oneself are both necessary.[44]

This again is something I explore in more detail elsewhere.[45]

Although Daoism is one of the smallest religions of all, we must not underestimate its influence. Tens of millions of people in China follow Daoist practices and millions more visit Daoist sacred sites and go on pilgrimages every year. Actually Daoism, like Buddhism, is more a philosophy of life than a religion, as Daoists worship no god as such. But they see in the deepening world environmental crisis that ways of human thinking have unbalanced the harmonious relationship between human beings and nature, and overstressed the power and influence of the human will over nature. The Daoist believes that nature has its own limits, that if recklessly exploited by greed or desire, we will see extinction and destruction. The number of thriving species on our planet measures the affluence of the true Daoist. If one considers the continuing destruction of life forms on this earth, the many species threatened with a man-induced extinction, then by Daoist standards we are now becoming very poor indeed.

And so we come finally to Christianity, a religion with a bad name when we consider how it has failed to serve nature in the past. This is a reputation we badly need to shake off. The problem has been that throughout the history of Christianity, its followers have tended to think of their relationship with God's Divine creation in terms of stewardship, based on the use of the term 'dominion' in biblical translations: which has been too often interpreted as mastery. The good news is that faced by the threat of environmental crises, the main Christian Churches have been redefining their theology, although it seems to me that this has not been widely publicized or understood. A meeting of the World Council of Churches in Granavollen, Norway, as long ago as 1988 agreed that:

> The drive to have 'mastery' over creation has resulted in the senseless exploitation of natural resources, the alienation of the land from people and the destruction of indigenous cultures... Creation came into being by the will and love of the Triune God, and as such it possesses an inner cohesion and goodness. Though human eyes may not always discern it, every creature and the whole creation in chorus bear witness to the glorious unity and harmony with which creation is endowed. And when our human eyes are opened and our tongues unloosed, we too learn to praise and participate in the life, love, power and freedom that is God's continuing gift and grace.

The World Council of Churches came together again in 1990 "to consider the issues of justice, peace, and the integrity of creation," when they wrote in an affirmation of faith:

> The integrity of creation has a social aspect that we recognize as peace with justice, and an ecological aspect which we recognize in the self-renewing, sustainable character of natural eco-systems. We will resist the claim that anything in creation is merely a resource for human exploitation. We will resist species extinction for human benefit; consumerism and harmful mass production; pollution of land, air and waters; all human activities which are now leading to probable rapid climate change; and the policies and plans which contribute to the disintegration of creation.

The report concludes with a challenge to all Christians, "to discover anew the truth that God's love and liberation is for all creation, not just humanity; to realize that we should have been stewards, priests, co-creators with God for the rest of creation but have actually often been the ones responsible for its destruction; and to seek new ways of living and being Christians that will restore that balance and give the hope of life to so much of the endangered planet."[46]

Did this challenge filter down to the congregations of any church near you? Did we see it mentioned in the media? No! Christians now need to rise to that challenge, working alongside the other great religions that share similar views.

Hospitality

We all love entertaining others. We love sitting down together to a good meal, sharing perhaps a bottle of wine if our faith allows. In good company, what more could we ask for? We all need each other. The total hermit is a rare person indeed.

While hospitality is deeply rooted in Judeo-Christian tradition, it is also an essential part of most if not all religions. Throughout the Holy Bible the sharing of food together is often mentioned as a token of friendship and commitment. This entire code of hospitality in the Middle East was so strong that it is expressed in a biblical warning, never to neglect showing hospitality to strangers, "for thereby some have entertained angels unawares."[47] And of course Jesus shared his Last Supper with his Disciples before his Crucifixion and Resurrection. Christians celebrate this meal in the Holy Eucharist.

Such hospitality is fundamentally important to Muslims. It defines who they are and they judge themselves and each other on the generosity of their welcome to strangers as well as friends.[48]

Sikh hospitality is grounded in the 500 year old tradition of langar, which is the free distribution of vegetarian food to both rich and poor, regardless of caste, color, religion or status.[49]

Hindu culture also believes that appropriate hospitality

should be offered to any visitor to the home, even to an enemy. After all, they say, "A tree does not deny its shade even to the one who comes to cut it down."[50] The uninvited guest should be treated as good as God, says the popular Hindu proverb.

So we see that there are plenty of features common to our various beliefs, which we can acknowledge and should be celebrating. Let's also do all we can to understand and respect our differences.

But first a word of caution is needed.

I am a botanist. As a child I loved collecting and identifying and pressing the many flowering plants around the farm. But as they were pressed and dried they soon lost their color, and beauty and became simply scientific specimens for further study at a later date. The thrill was in finding new flowers, or discovering something fresh and exciting about an old familiar favorite.

I also love second-hand bookshops. Nothing, not even Amazon's 'marketplace', or the digital book, can replace the thrill of browsing shelves of old books and finding something new and relevant to whatever I may be researching at the time. That is how I stumbled upon A.C. Bouquet's *Comparative Religion*.

"No doubt the study has its dangers," writes Bouquet of his work (which would be rather more accurately described as 'the comparative study of religions'):[51] "It may sink to the level of collecting dead insects or pressed flowers, which in the process lose all their colour and reality. Collecting religions is no better. The only tolerable way of engaging in the work is to *let one's self be enthralled by man's ceaseless quest for something supernatural and eternal which the ordinary life of this world will never give him, and to try to put one's self into the place of those who are obviously enthusiasts for a religion which is not one's own*" (my emphasis).

Rowan Williams, as Archbishop of Canterbury, explained on his visit to the new Hindu Temple of Shri Venkateswara (Balaji) when it opened in Birmingham: "interfaith dialogue is not a way of obliterating our differences, it's a way of living creatively with them. A way of living gratefully with them, so that our compassion, our love and our fellow feeling do not stop simply with those who are like us."

Wisdom dynamics

Of course our classic ancient texts and the spiritual wisdom they embody should never be seen as beyond criticism. But to what extent should we use them as a rulebook by the faithful for 21st century living? In his book *Let There be Light*, Skolimowski argues that wisdom is "a set of dynamic structures: always to be re-built, re-structured, re-adjusted, re-articulated... Past spiritual traditions, of nearly all religions, have so often insisted that the wisdom they offer is absolute, while it is only temporary. For all wisdom is historical and evolving, including the so-called religious wisdom."[52]

But this seems to be too much of a generalization. Skolimowski is surely not dismissing all ancient wisdom as valueless in today's world.

The study of textual interpretation or hermeneutics is a massive subject, trying as it does through various techniques to arrive at the author's intended meaning. But it's also an endlessly fascinating subject. Factors such as the cultural and historical setting of the work, the way words are used and their context within the complete script may all play a part in interpretation, and there is plenty of scope for different viewpoints on any particular text.

So of course we must be critical, but not necessarily dismissive of our ancient wisdoms. Some less well-known, even largely forgotten wisdoms could have universal significance for humanity today if we would only listen to their message. Let's take one example.

When the Israelites entered Canaan in the 14th century BC the land was carved up between them per capita, and the Jubilee Land Laws were written.[53] No freehold sales were allowed and every 50th year, the Jubilee Year, the land had to revert to the original family freeholder,[54] at which time the people were to return to their own clans.[55] At this same time bonded servants or debt slaves were released. This welfare system may sound generous and impractical to us today, but it ensured that the disabled, elderly and infirm were cared for, and the extended family was kept together, maintaining personal dignity and self-reliance for all. That sounds very good to me.

Then there were the laws that gave freedom from debt servitude. There was an interest ban on loans between Israelites (although not applicable to refugees and immigrants) and the loan would be cancelled every seven years. This kept the wealth within a family unit and worked to keep the family together. Again surely not a bad idea?

Lending was about helping the poor and needy through financial crises. Loans were for helping in the short-term; they were not intended to cause any hardship to a borrower over the longer term.

These laws for periodic debt cancellation and the return of family property protected a family's roots and avoided wealth concentration and economic dependency. The laws underlined justice on the one hand with redistribution rules and the importance of relationships on the other, with families being rooted in their own areas. "There is hope for your future, says the Lord, and your children shall come back to their own country."[56]

In the global economic crises of this new century, perhaps some of the wisdom of these ancient Jubilee Land Laws and rules as to debt forgiveness and usury, found in the *Holy Bible* books of Leviticus and Joshua, could offer the basis of a different model for our banking system and land ownership in our Western economy.[57] Our current system encourages global mobility in the workforce, which brings with it the inherent disadvantages of losing family cohesion, not knowing others around you in society and not feeling part of any community. When people generally do not feel loyalty and attachment to a particular area there can be an increase in crimes against the person and an increase in violence against the environment.

In Islamic Shari'a law there is a prohibition on charging interest on loans, a practice they regard as usury. Aristotle made the distinction between essential and therefore laudable expenditure for the daily needs of food, shelter and clothing, and the acquisition of money for acquisition's sake by profit associated with retail trade. The latter he censured:

> ...because the gain in which it results is not naturally made, but is made at the expense of other men. The trade of the petty usurer is hated with most reason: it makes a profit from currency itself, instead of making it from the process which currency was meant to serve. Currency came into existence merely as a means of exchange; usury tries to make it increase.[58]

Avoiding usurious loans helped Islamic banks to survive the early 21st century crash of the other big banks run on conventional Western lines.

Bankers take note!

Let's take another example. We have a problem when religions believe they hold the only path to truth; and we are in a mess because of this. The Shinto masters say: "My truth does not need to be the same as your truth." And this is also the Jain way. We can all be right, in different ways. We can respect the other point of view totally, and find common factors, connecting strands, between otherwise conflicting arguments. This is the ancient Jain idea of Anekant, non-violence of the mind, or Many Sided Wisdom, explained in a book of the same name by Aidan Rankin.[59] It requires us to recondition our minds; to change the way we look at ideas. Jains have a fundamental respect and sympathy with all creatures. All life is interconnected, and they believe our intelligence confers responsibility, not entitlement. They understand each individual as a unit of consciousness. We are all on a spiritual journey, they say, but we are restricted by our human consciousness that is not fully evolved spiritually. Rankin is at pains to explain that while his book is based on Jainism the concept is relevant within the practice of all religions and across all religious divides. Indeed, an increasing number of people are sensing a shift in consciousness towards a greater spirituality in today's world as envisioned by the Jains.

Heeding such ancient wisdom, a wisdom that has surely survived the test of time, could transform individuals and society, and the world in which we live, offering the path to a safer better world for all humanity. Anekant, Rankin tells us, is a gift from Jainism to the world, and if allowed to do so, it has the potential to heal not only our wounded planet but also the wounds within ourselves. It is a gift we would all do well to use gratefully and with humility and understanding.

Other religions teach similar ideas. The Sikhs teach that all the religions of the world can be compared to rivers flowing into a single ocean. Sikhism believes that humans have the freedom to find their own path to salvation, a popular sticking point among those who want to be critical rather than constructive in inter-faith dialogue.

Judaism holds that God has entered into a covenant with all mankind, and that Jews and non-Jews alike have a relationship with God.

Central to the Bahá'í belief is the unity of all humanity within diversity, and that all people are created equal and are valued in God's sight regardless of religion, color or race, and that they should all love the whole world. Skolimowski views all of this in the context of "many different paths around the Mountain of Enlightenment, leading to its peaks."[60]

I know that not everyone reading this will agree but I am quite happy in my own mind that there can be different paths to the same transcendent reality. I like the story of Senator Quintus Aurelius Symmachus (c. 345–402), a Roman statesman, orator, and man of letters in fourth century Rome, addressing the Emperor Valentinian II, in defense of paganism and the restoration of the statue of the goddess Victoria in the Roman Senate:

> It is the same thing that we all worship; we all think the same; we look up to the same stars; there is one sky above us, one world around us; what difference does it make with what kind of method the individual seeks the truth? We cannot all follow the same path to so great a mystery.[61]

We all have a duty of care to the world, whether based upon our sensitivity and compassion or the beliefs of our religions, or indeed both. We surely have to look beyond our own horizons more and appreciate our place in a much wider world. We need to live, and let live.

As the Sikh teaches us:

> All life is interconnected. A human body consists of many parts; every one of them has a distinct name, location, and function, and all of them are dependent upon each other. In the same way, all the constituents of this universe and this earth are dependent upon each other. Decisions in one country or continent cannot be ignored by others. Choices in one place have measurable consequences for the rest of the world. It is part of the same system.[62]

Why is that so very hard to understand and live up to? Gandhi believed in the fundamental Truth of all the great religions of the world:

> I believe they are all God given and I believe they were

necessary for the people to whom these religions were revealed. And I believe that if only we could all of us read the scriptures of the different faiths from the standpoint of the followers of these faiths, we should find that they were at the bottom all one and were all helpful to one another.[63]

Mehta says the same thing in a slightly different way:

The word of the different scriptures presents wide disagreements and also intimate harmonies. All these throw light on each other. And if only our eyes have been well washed by the tears of our heart's longing for Truth, we shall see its wonderful richness displayed in the variety of its expressions, and we may understand any and every religion all the better for it.[64]

Let's listen to ancient wisdoms and the wisdom of great philosophers and statesmen, and let's use the many features and beliefs that are common to all the faiths and religions as opportunities for building bridges, as threads to bring and bind faiths together in a common purpose. And let's recognize the immense and positive roles that religions are variously playing on the world stage towards building a better world for us all.

There really is so much that is positive about religions. It seems vitally important now more than ever that these things are fully understood, that prejudices built on ignorance can be silenced, that differences can be put aside, that past wrongs can be forgiven and forgotten and that all can pull together, the religious, the atheists, the 'spiritual but not religious' and the agnostics, in fact everyone, for the future good of all mankind and for creation, whether or not we believe it was created by a Higher Being.

Unfortunately good news does not make good news in media terms, and sadly religion is too often highlighted for what is bad.

And this then colors the way we think of religion. Religion is not the main cause of wars, terrorism, and other violent episodes, and it is not in terminal decline. And our deeds of compassion and love to our fellow men are not done as desperate acts in our death throes, or simply to gain a place in Heaven, or both. It's time to look at some of the reasons given by those who will have nothing whatsoever to do with religion or faith and try to dispel some of these common and misleading notions.

Chapter 3

Why Not Religion? The Main Obstacles to Understanding

Faith is believing what we know ain't true.
Mark Twain

In 2011 there was dissent and fury among American Creationist Christians. Professor John Schneider was forced to retire from Calvin College in Michigan, a Christian university, because he suggested that it was becoming ever harder to believe literally in Adam and Eve, and the concept of Original Sin and the Garden of Eden.

The atheists and the media, anxious to illustrate the continuing stupidity of so many Christians who won't allow men such as Schneider to honestly develop their thoughts and speak their minds without sacrificing their careers, pounce upon stories such as this.

Strengthened by advances in genetic science and molecular biology, the scientific evidence for evolution by natural selection is now very strong, although there are still gaps and uncertainties to address. None of us have all the answers.

Charles Darwin introduced his theory of evolution through natural selection in 1859. By 1880 it was no longer particularly controversial, and had gained widespread support both in America and in Britain among educated Christians, aided by committed Christian scientists and theologians on both sides of the Atlantic, including many of the early Christian 'fundamentalists'.[65]

It is only relatively recently that Darwin's ideas have been scorned, sometimes passionately, by an increasing number of

Creationists, New Creationists and most recently by the proponents of Intelligent Design. The original 1920s Creationism was simply anti-Darwin and ran out of steam with the death of William Bryan, the movement's passionate campaigner. But in the 1960s a new variant was born, within the Young Earth Creationists, who teach that the earth is less than 10,000 years old and that God created all things in six literal 24-hour days. Nearly half of Americans seemingly hold to this anti-Darwinian belief. It would now seem that the UK is catching up. In the land where Darwin lived and worked, perhaps only a quarter of his fellow countrymen accept him and his ideas beyond any reasonable doubt.[66]

The great irony is that in putting forward the idea so robustly that evolution is selfish, robotic, pointless, mechanical and indeed Godless (ideas that are not only bleak but also contested even in scientific circles), the Neo Darwinists with an atheist agenda quite simply seem to have turned more Christians and others away from Darwinism and towards alternative and possibly less credible ideas of Creation and the origins of life. And these alternative belief systems are the very same that the neo atheists use to mock and deride the religious among us, for our obvious stupidity. The atheists cannot believe the supposed ignorance of the followers of a faith based as they see it on fairy tales and myths. Which in itself ignores the provenance of many of the sacred texts and the fact that biblical studies and theological interpretation are constantly developing disciplines. Science continually moves on to further theories and discoveries in much the same way. And what is wrong with myths anyway? "Myths are the mirrors in which we can study human life," wrote the psychotherapist Petruska Clarkson.[67] Of course another great irony that comes out of all this is that both the 'militant godless' and the 'militant Godly' see evolution as respectively denying or threatening any belief in God.

There is a huge misconception here that science and religion are in competition over the question of evolution and where we all come from. Darwin didn't see things that way at all. He was always thoughtful about the possible problems with his theory of evolution by natural selection, and was equally clear that it did not make atheism inevitable. "It seems to me absurd to doubt that a man may be an ardent Theist and an evolutionist," he wrote towards the end of his life.[68] He was never an atheist himself, going from Christianity to theism to agnosticism during his lifetime. But he was always courteous and respectful to anyone who disagreed with his views, willing always to listen openly to other ideas. Now we could do with much more of that kind of dialogue, sadly missing in many of our debates and conversations today. This leads us to the next big question.

Are religion and science incompatible?

After all, if there is no God, then God is incalculably the greatest single creation of the human imagination.
Sir Anthony John Patrick Kenny, Fellow of the British Academy
I only know that I know nothing.
Socrates

When Edgar Mitchell, Apollo 14 astronaut and the sixth man on the moon, saw the cosmos and the earth for the first time from space he wrote: "My view of our planet was a glimpse of divinity... we went to the moon as technicians; we returned as humanitarians."[69] Many astronauts, all highly trained scientists or technicians and dependent on the latest most complex technology for their missions, have, like Mitchell, found a spiritual awakening or deepened their particular religious faith when in awe and reverence they have seen the earth from a different perspective, from space.

Scientific experimental methods simply suggest probabilities, from experiments devised to test theories: nothing more or less.

I think many misunderstand this; they misunderstand how science operates, what it sets out to achieve, and fail to understand the lack of any total certainty in much of science. The Dalai Lama warns us that we should not "overlook the limitations of science. In replacing religion as the final source of knowledge in popular estimation, science begins to look a bit like another religion itself. With this comes a similar danger on the part of some of its adherents to blind faith in its principles, and, correspondingly, to intolerance of alternate views."[70] "What a wonderful, what a religious discipline, is science and mathematics. Today science has shown me that all that is discovered is only an approximate knowing, and that I cannot even reach, let alone touch or overstep the frontiers of knowledge..." These were the wise words of Phiroz Dorabji Mehta (1 October 1902–2 May 1994) an Indian brought up in the Zarathushtrian[71] religion who wrote and lectured on religious topics, studied natural sciences at Cambridge and pursued many other interests, including astronomy, poetry and philosophy. He was a polymath in the true sense of the word.

In his wonderful book *The Heart of Religion*, written over a period of 20 years, Mehta brought 50 years of study and practice together to explore what it means to understand and live the religious life, to evolve towards a life that is "free from fear, greed and hatred, a life in which our actions are pure, wise and compassionate."

He further wrote: "For him who attempts to write about the deeps of religion, science is a powerful aid, for the scientific discipline helps in curing the mind of intellectual cobweb-spinning, of using misleading analogies and of false reasoning." He went on to observe that science has become a god for many, a modern idol! (This was in 1976 – we do not seem to have learned!) "Applied science, technology, holds the human race in thrall to the machine. Drugs, chemicals and various inventions destroy man and nature alike and fill the plundered Earth with pollution.

Mankind, perhaps all life on the globe, is in danger of extermination by man. No animal has shown such ingratitude to Life. Vast hordes senselessly look to technology to solve human problems and produce human fulfillment."[72]

From talking with delegates at the many conferences I attend, with scientists, doctors, philosophers and scholars from many disciplines, I know I'm far from alone in my belief that science, religion and spirituality are not mutually exclusive.[73] If we are prepared to take a dialectical look at the extremes of polarity between the scientific and the spiritual viewpoints, between the objective and the subjective, between thinking and feeling, the expressible and the ineffable, between our outer or exoteric selves and the inner or esoteric, we may be able to appreciate that these extremes are simply different ways of viewing the same reality.

We have inherited the works of the great mystics, from all cultures and faiths. They have seen things, experienced things, which they have been able to articulate for the benefit of us all. And many of us are able to feel these qualities from both a heart and a head perspective, to have a sense of the spiritual, the intrinsic, the inner, as well as an ability to analyze rationally and objectively.

In spite of all this, many now seem to believe that science and religion are entirely incompatible, at opposite ends of the spectrum of understanding. Western civilization and education and the advance of scientific knowledge has without doubt brought us many wonderful achievements but sometimes the costs are unwelcome. Such 'progress' could also spell disaster, sitting as we do on too many weapons of mass destruction, and with some countries in the developing world simply awash with guns and armory. The great problem is that within this culture is the seemingly prevalent view that science answers all our questions, or will do so if we are prepared to wait long enough. And the most fundamentalist atheists tell us that if science is going to provide all our answers, there is no further need for religion in our lives.

But science was after all originally called the natural philosophy. It is only relatively recently that its meaning has been hijacked by the reductionist scientists and the angry atheists for their own agenda. The brilliant, creative and innovative biologist Rupert Sheldrake calls for scientists to look beyond the rigid materialistic dogma that they have built their discipline around. Echoing the words of the Dalai Lama, Sheldrake says that this scientific worldview has become a belief system in its own right, that we should be questioning some of its assumptions and looking at the world with new eyes and a more open mind. We need to challenge the belief that all reality is material or physical, that the world is a machine made up only of dead matter, that minds and memories are locked within our brains.[74]

Mitchell went on to found the Institute of Noetic Sciences, an organization that "conducts and sponsors leading-edge research into the potentials and powers of consciousness, including perceptions, beliefs, attention, intention, and intuition." The Institute is committed to scientific rigor while at the same time it explores phenomena that do not necessarily fit conventional scientific models.[75] For example it includes among its many current research projects a study of how engagement in spiritual practices is related to health and well-being.[76]

Science has a very long way to go before it can hope to fully explain our inner worlds of human consciousness and spirituality. I believe that it will be Sheldrake's kind of science that will bring us the most exciting advances in understanding our brain and our consciousness. Far from reinforcing ideas of incompatibility with religion, a new science may even begin to bridge the gap between science on the one hand, and religion and spirituality on the other. I shall explore these ideas later alongside some possibly controversial ideas of my own on the science/religion interface.

Physicists are far more at home than biologists with the uncertainties of our world, our cosmos, and our consciousness. Einstein trumped Newton with his special theory of relativity, which says that an object cannot travel faster than the speed of light. In 2011 scientists at the world's largest physics laboratory at CERN (the European Organization for Nuclear Research) thought they had found evidence to suggest that subatomic particles were indeed capable of traveling faster than the speed of light[77] and this caused great media and scientific excitement for a while. Just a few months later some issues were found with the equipment used in the experiment and the results had to be reappraised.

The truth is that we simply don't know what we do not know. "Whereof one cannot speak, thereof one must be silent," wrote Wittgenstein.[78] As Chris Clarke writes in *Weaving the Cosmos: Science, Religion and Ecology*: "the realm of the unprovable will forever outstrip our attempts to grasp it."[79]

Science clearly expands knowledge, and contributes to a more compassionate world through its many positive discoveries and inventions. But as Paul Gilbert reminds us in *The Compassionate Mind*, it is not helpful for the majority of people on this planet if we use scientific knowledge "to demolish [their] belief systems, leaving them with nothing other than the lives they have been born into."[80]

Dave Tomlinson was a former influential leader in the House Church movement until he became disillusioned with its approach to spirituality and theology, especially in the charismatic church. In his book *Re-Enchanting Christianity: Faith in an Emerging Culture*, Tomlinson is clear that there is no intrinsic conflict between science and faith.[81] But we have to ask the right questions: how do we interpret the Bible to make sense of it in a scientific age, how do we make sense of a creedal faith drawn up within a different culture?

In 1999 Richard Dawkins said that it was his "suspicion...

hunch... and hope" that within the 21st century the nature of the "mysterious substance called consciousness", that "spiritual part of man regarded as surviving after death, the theory that there is something non-material about life, some non-physical vital principle... vital force... mysterious energy or... spirit,"[82] will be completely mastered by scientific explanation and the soul will be definitely dispatched once and for all. With the same reasoning he argues passionately that there can be no God.[83] Quite apart from the muddled lumping together of consciousness, spirit, soul, vital force, energy, life after death, and more, with a possibly flawed and misplaced certainty that they all mean the same thing, this reductionist thinking does our world no favors.

In response to this, I can do no better than quote Nobel Laureate Sir Peter Medawar, in his 1979 book *Advice to a Young Scientist*:[84] "There is no quicker way for a scientist to bring discredit upon himself and upon his profession than roundly to declare – particularly when no declaration of any kind is called for – that science knows, or soon will know, the answers to all questions worth asking..." I suspect Richard Dawkins has not read Medawar.

The fact is that Dawkins' "hunch" is fast losing its credibility. An increasing number of respected and eminent scientists and philosophers, Sheldrake included, are challenging those who only see the human being in terms of physical body and brain. There really is something more to life than mere matter, something that is perhaps for the moment beyond the ability of scientists to prove or disprove empirically. God most certainly is not dead.[85] But there are many who do not seem to realize this.[86]

John Polkinghorne, the eminent English theoretical physicist, theologian, writer and Anglican Priest, as well as a Fellow of the Royal Society, defends theology, like science, as being an "investigation of what is, the search for increasing verisimilitude in our understanding of reality." In his book *One World: The Interaction of Science and Theology,* he explains that theological enquiry is based on scripture, tradition and reason.[87] He defends the idea that science and theology both explore aspects of reality. It is just that they are concerned with different levels of meaning. Science, he points out, uses the quantitative language of math, while religion uses the qualitative language of symbols.[88]

There is a real need for us all to show much more humility and be far more open-minded to the coexistence of science with the religious and the spiritual as well as the secular. We need all of these in the world, cooperating in an atmosphere of mutual respect and understanding. We need balance between the head and the heart.

And unless and until more people realize this truth, then both God and religion are in for a hard time; and that bodes ill for the future of the world.

Why is my wisdom better than your wisdom?

Christians are often criticized as arrogant, especially when they insist that they alone hold the Truth, that they provide the only path to salvation, with the oft quoted 'no one comes to the Father except by me' approach to their faith. This can make them dismissive of other religious beliefs. They either do not take them seriously, or regard them as ripe for evangelism and conversion. Joseph Ratzinger, now Pope Benedict XVI, in his book *Truth and Tolerance: Christian Belief and World Religions,* tackles this enormously complex theological debate in some considerable depth. Abrahamic scriptures, he tells us, offer two attitudes to other faiths. They are "either provisional, precursors of Christianity, on the road to enlightenment, or they are insufficient, anti-Christian, contrary to truth..." This does little to improve the image of Christianity, although he attempts some kind of a reconciliation with other religions through considering them as ultimately all being on the same historical path towards enlightenment; "that we are all a part of a single history that is in many different fashions on the way toward God..."[89]

In fact there are a very large number of religious moderates across the world, who do not see their faith as the only way to Truth. In the United States it seems that the majority now accept other religious truths besides their own.[90] And the Archbishop of Canterbury Rowan Williams, speaking to the World Council of Churches, while referring to the Christian faith as being uniquely fulfilling to its followers, said that this should not prevent Christians from recognizing elements of ultimate truth in other religions, or from listening carefully to others with respect, and with the willingness to collaborate.[91] Elsewhere Williams has further explained his thinking thus:

> although we have a history that is sometimes one of conflict and rivalry, we have begun slowly but steadily to develop that much richer vision which allows us to say we help one another to be human in our difference. And because our religious identities are not just something that affects one little part of our lives but something that has to do with the most profound and definitive relationships that we have, our relationship to God, to reality, that surely is a reason for not seeing our religious belonging, our religious identity, as ever in competition with other things but rather as the context in which all our thinking, all our loving and all our hoping takes place.[92]

War

One of the most common reasons given for not wanting anything to do with religion is that religions cause most of our wars. But do they?

Excuses abound for war and violence without any need for religion at all! The religions' historian, Karen Armstrong, in her book *The Case for God*, shows us that wars are more about greed, envy and ambition, cloaked perhaps in religious rhetoric to give them 'respectability.' And they can certainly be fuelled by religious difference.[93] But we are also attached to too many possessions, and Aidan Rankin[94] claims that it is this attachment, rather than religion per se, that is the cause of so many wars that are too often blamed exclusively on religion. It is true that many conflicts are fought over geographical boundaries, hypothetical lines drawn on maps, although religious passions do run deep when that land or property is sacred.

For many people the religious Crusades come first to mind. Yes they were bloody, and the reasons behind them enormously complex; basically they were great military expeditions undertaken by the Christian nations of Europe for the purpose of rescuing the holy places of Palestine from the hands of the Mohammedans. But here again we are talking about the fight for possession of land and property,

In Gustav Niebuhr's book *Beyond Tolerance*, he refers to a night in 1993 when there were 40 wars going on in the world, but on analysis most of them were fuelled rather than caused by religion.

However, it is indisputable that we now live in a more perilous world than those of us who are children of the 1950s could possibly have foreseen. There are more wars worldwide than ever before. It is true that in the Western world many of us have experienced unbroken peace since the end of the Second World War. But we can no longer ignore the wider global picture. In those terms the future is bleaker, with so much war and civil unrest obvious from our daily news. But what is really causing this unrest if it is not religion? A moment's reflection tells us that hunger, injustice, inequalities and tyrant dictators play a significant part. We witnessed in 2011 the most extraordinary events that have been collectively called the Arab Spring. Were not these uprisings more about injustice and inequality and tyrannical rule than about religion? It is quite likely that wars of the future will be similarly caused. Researchers have also found that environmental shifts are already contributing to war and strife and we can expect further displacement of refugees through climate change in the future that will threaten peace in the areas affected. "If you have social inequality, people are poor, and there are underlying tensions, it seems possible that climate can deliver the knockout punch."[95] And religions work tirelessly to address the causes of these tensions.

So perhaps instead of endlessly debating the role of religion in past and indeed current wars we should concentrate on how the religious – and for that matter atheists and humanists – can peaceably coexist. Remember the common features: the Golden Rule; the rules that call for universal love and that forbid killing; the common concern for Creation; the notion of hospitality.

But since violence and intolerance are linked with religious fundamentalism in the minds of many, let's briefly look at that next.

Fundamentalism

The original meaning of fundamentalism has been hijacked from a movement spawned from Protestant disagreements in early 20th century America. Certain Presbyterians of the day protested against the scientific progress of the time including the new Darwinian evolution theory, promoting instead their strongly held view that the Bible represents literal historical truth, as to the creation of the world, for example. These so-called fundamental truths of Christianity were published in a series of pamphlets, *The Fundamentals*. Hence the name of a movement was born that has now gathered such negative 21st century connotations. Religious fundamentalism has been described by Niebuhr as "an elastic term lately stretched to cover a vast variety of militant tendencies including violence," but the province of only a small, if significant, minority.[96]

Fundamentalism need not always be a threat to freedom and tolerance. The Jains and the Amish are themselves fundamentalists, although largely speaking in a good or positive way.[97] But ask any man in the street what he means by religious fundamentalism and words like intolerance and violence will almost certainly spring to his mind. This perception is fuelled by articulate atheists such as Dawkins, Hitchens and Harris, for example, who tend to focus on the militant fundamentalist aspects of modern religion, as if they are an essential part of mainstream religious belief, although this of course is not so.[98] Nonetheless, that "significant minority" cannot be ignored; it is claimed that they are "better organized, more experienced, better coordinated, and more motivated [than the religious majority]. They have more stratagems, more institutes, more people, more money, more power, more influence."[99] And it is certainly true that there are potentially dangerous fundamentalists in all the world's major religions.

Nowhere is the tension greater than between the great Abrahamic religions of Islam and Christianity. One poll shows that 60% of Christians are prejudiced against Muslims and 30% of Muslims are prejudiced against Christians.[100] There is a great deal of mutual misunderstanding and fear between Muslims and Christians born firstly out of ignorance and secondly out of the painful memories of past wrongs inflicted on each other through a fairly bloody history; especially those Crusades. But ignorance needs to be counteracted by education and a supportive, responsible and cooperative media. Past wrongs call for mutual forgiveness, so that both religions may move on towards a more peaceful coexistence. How this may be achieved I shall return to in more detail later.

Surely we should be able to learn from the past, be more mature in our thinking and learn to enter dialogue before resorting to violence? Shouldn't we have grown up? But when grievances, suspicion and distrust run deep, as they do within the hearts of many Muslims and Christians, we have an explosive mix.

And then, as already seen, increased competition for scarce resources, for example, could be all that is needed to ignite smoldering passions into dreadful violence. The dangers are obvious.

Let's look at a further criticism leveled against the religious.

The religious are stupid or ignorant or both

The popular atheist writers continually levy this criticism against the religious. As a scientific research postgraduate by background, with a First Class Honors degree, a PhD and several other professional qualifications to my name, I resent that! Also look at the credentials of many of our most eminent scientists who believe in God, for example Dr Francis Collins, the director of the Human Genome Project, and the theoretical physicist and Anglican priest John Polkinghorne KBE, FRS. From the past, we can add many famous scientists to the list, including for example Albert Einstein, Max Planck, Michael Faraday, Sir Francis Bacon, Isaac Newton, Rene Descartes and Galileo Galilei.[101]

When Barack Obama became President of the United States 10% of Americans thought that he was a Muslim. Apparently nearly 20% or one in five now hold that view.[102] He is, in fact, a practicing and devout Christian. Ignorance, and particularly ignorance about religions, is a serious world problem. But this is an ignorance shared by atheists and the religious alike.

The anger and the 'war on terror' in the immediate aftermath of the events of 9/11 were almost certainly prompted by a misguided fear fuelled by ignorance. Its very connotation assumes a 'them and us', and often by 'them' we mean Muslims. This has therefore become a serious obstacle to acceptance, tolerance or respect.

Ignorance is dangerous because it supports a misunderstanding, or a suspicion, of the 'other' point of view. And this often fuels fear, and fear fuels general ridicule or worse. Thus Herod ordered the slaying of the Holy Innocents because of his fear that his power was being usurped by the birth of the boy Jesus "born to be King."

Ignorance is a two-way street. Criticisms of religion often say more about the ignorance, lack of education or simply muddled knowledge of the critic than about the realities of the religion itself, and such ignorance poses a serious obstacle to religious understanding and tolerance.

Let's face it. The arguments of the atheists and humanists are tired. They tend to trash religion on dogmatic statements of the faith that are sometimes barely recognizable to present day believers. All such stories tell us, more often than not, is that there is a need for much more education about the many different religions and faiths. We need to teach, not attack!

During an interview with Jon Stewart of the American program *The Daily Show*,[103] the popular non-fiction writer and professed atheist Sam Harris explained that the motivating factor for writing his book *The Moral Landscape: How Science can Determine Human Values* was what he described as the problem of having only "religious demagogues who think the planet is 6,000-years-old" as the source of morality in today's world. It's almost impossible to find reliable statistics, but it would seem from a trawl of the Internet that in America, where the Christian Creationists are mostly congregated, "only about one-third [of the population] today believes the Bible is absolutely accurate and that it should be taken literally word for word. The rest either feel that the Bible is the inspired word of God, but not literally so, or that it is a book of ancient fables, legends, and history as recorded by man."[104]

The following is another statement I found browsing the web that is fairly typical of biased or ignorant reporting where religion is concerned. "It is true of every so-called holy text in every religion today that no one has the slightest idea of who wrote them or even when they were written." Really? Of course not![105]

We cannot ignore some of the extreme religious rites and procedures, for example the cruelty of female circumcision that we know occurs in many countries. But again these are largely based on an ignorance that needs to be addressed. Grayling in *What is Good*[106] compares the Japanese secular appreciation of aesthetics (the prose he quotes from *In Praise of Shadows* by Junichiro Tanizaki certainly conveys well the natural beauty of the world and our spiritual experience of it) with the extreme story of the cruelty inflicted in the Christian Victorian England upbringing of one child. He tells us that this style of upbringing is still common throughout the world where religion plays a dominant role. Of course that is not strictly true; it is an overgeneralization. Sam Harris makes the point rather better in *The End of Faith*, calling for us to confront those societies "whose moral and political development – in their treatment of women and children, in their prosecution of war, in their approach to criminal justice, and in their intuitions about what constitutes cruelty – lags behind our own." But this is not to do with religion. This is to do with education and the process of civilization.

Ignorance needs to be countered with education. There is clearly much ignorance, fear and misunderstanding to be overcome surrounding the many different world religions. In today's world strident God-denouncing books are widely read, whereas serious and informative religious and spiritual material scarcely gets shelf room; because it fails the mantra: What's in it for the reader? We live in a quick sound-bite, low concentration, noisy, violent, opinionated world where every one looks only to his own interests; the 'spiritual' books that are read most widely are those that promise personal growth and development, or success and wealth. Welcome to the 'Me- Millennium'.

The media

If only the media had the will, they could be a part of that vitally important education process.

So much of what is in the public domain comes via the media, from TV and radio and newspapers, or their linked Internet sites, and is dispersed further through social networking and blogging sites. So the media have a huge responsibility to be truthful and unbiased in their reporting. Sadly there is often a massive bias against all things good that come out of religion.[107]

For example the minimal media coverage of the 2011 floods in Pakistan failed to mention the many Pakistani businessmen, largely Muslim, who put their companies on hold, often for many months, while they went to help in the afflicted areas.[108] And after 9/11 a Gallop Poll[109] showed that 93% of Muslims worldwide said that the atrocity was not justified, and none said that it was justified on religious grounds. The small number, 7%, who said 9/11 was justified quoted political reasons! Furthermore, most said the biggest obstacle to better relations with the West was the latter's lack of respect for Islam. How many knew that from media reports? And how do we generate respect for Islam, indeed for any faith, if we are widely ignorant of the facts surrounding that faith?

Niebuhr tells us that the media misrepresented what happened after 9/11. He says that the immediate response of the citizens of New York was to preserve their community, to look after the vulnerable, to show neighborliness, to demonstrate that all were in this tragedy together, not pitching one against another as a 'war on terror' implies. There was a strong sense of responsibility and humanity demonstrated across all faiths and cultures. Furthermore, he writes, and despite what the media reported, that the event generated a hunger for more information and understanding of Islam, through dialogue with Muslim neighbors.[110] A social and intellectual response was called for, as much as a military one. How much of that was covered by the media?[111]

We have to demand better media, because the media is so invasive into our consciousness, so easy to tap into through the

Internet, almost impossible to avoid, so difficult to assess objectively, and yet so powerful and far-reaching in its influence. The creative forces at work in the media that relentlessly bring so many images into our lives, the writers, editors, journalists, photographers and all the myriad of support staff we see listed for example in the credits at the end of any film, bear an awesome responsibility.

There is so much good going on at local, national and international level but the media prefer to report on the bad. And they are quite clearly biased against inter-religious dialogue.

A few years ago I attended an event aimed to bring Muslims and Christians together for a day of dialogue and fellowship. It was heavily attended, from parishes and mosques around the district, and a useful day was had. On arrival we were surprised by the large gathering of police outside the venue, clearly expecting trouble! There was none. There was no story therefore for the media, and as far as I could ascertain the event was not covered locally or nationally. Would that have been different if there had been any violence? But then again why should there have been any? And good news is no news.

As is the case with all human creativity, those working in the media can use their talents to help bridge any rifts and help heal the world, or to assist subtly in keeping wounds open. We all have free will and choice. The choice of direction is ours.

Of course we have seen that not everything about all religions is good. We have to be critical or we slip into a dangerous relativism. Take the caste system within Hinduism, the violence seen within Islam and Christianity, all negative and degenerative aspects of otherwise great faiths.

But we achieve nothing by accentuating the negative, pouring ridicule on the idea of God, or by calling for the abolition of religion, an impossible idea.

Why is religion often seen as an evil force, or just simply a 'bad thing' when we could celebrate instead its diversity and virtues? Why does it seem so often to be the victim of ridicule or worse? Unfortunately it is all too common for atheists to trash faith or religion on dogmatic statements of the faith that are barely recognizable to the religious believer. For example A.C. Grayling in *What is Good* scorns the religious with disdain and bias verging on an apparent ignorance that seems unlikely given his education and background. My life as a Christian, apparently, is totally dictated by self-interest, my good deeds are done not from any motive of altruism or compassion, but to avoid the posthumous punishment of hell and damnation in an afterlife, and in return for the reward of "eternal bliss." Really? This is not the faith I recognize, nor I imagine the faith recognized by many others. And then Grayling goes further to say that our good works are the cry of a religion in decline. The claim of the contemporary churches that they support charity and help the people of Third World countries in their distresses, demonstrating peace, kindness, brotherly love and charitable works, is the "soft face" of the church, he writes, displayed to the world when we are on the "back-foot", a minority interest looking to recruit, primarily among the lonely, the desperate, the timid. When we come from a position of strength, he says, things are very different, witness the Inquisition and the Taliban, for example.[112] I suppose on that basis I cannot really win any argument here because any attempt by me to try to live my life true to Christ's teaching, or to urge support of other religions in their good work, is a desperate attempt by me to salvage dying religions and gain brownie points for a heavenly eternity!

Atheists such as Dawkins who try to rubbish religion through the mantra of materialistic science apparently fail to appreciate the limitations of this way of viewing the world, blind to other possibilities.

The portrayal and perception of religions have much to do with media bias. It is certainly true that religions must adapt to the changing needs of the 21st century. But to portray religion as a minority interest in terminal decline is inaccurate to say the least, taking the global perspective.

I firmly believe that we must not dismiss religion lightly and carelessly. I have already shown some of the many ways that religion is a force for good in the world, and why we should be nurturing and supporting religion, not baying for its abolition. Now I shall explore the substantial and important work being done in fostering more inter-religious tolerance, before looking at the whole question of spirituality and religion, and then putting forward an idea or two of my own.

Chapter 4

Tolerance and Beyond

Those who praise their own doctrines and disparage the doctrines of others do not solve any problem.
Jainism. *Sutrakritanga 1.1.50*
Why may we not suppose that the great Father of all is pleased with a variety of devotion?
Thomas Paine: *The Rights of Man*[113]

I've just come back from watching 17 small rowing boats set off across the Atlantic for the West Indies from La Gomera in the Canary Islands, a distance of 2550 nautical miles. Some are rowing single-handed (that in itself being a huge challenge mentally as well as physically) but most have a crew of 2, 4 or 6 people. It will certainly be grueling physically, but imagine sharing such a confined space with others for somewhere between 40 and 90 days, with no escape. However strong the bonds of friendship beforehand, this will test relationships to the utmost. And the men and women will have plenty of time to discover each other, before they see land again.

One person rocking the boat literally or metaphorically may seriously affect the rest of the crew. They will have to learn tolerance in a big way, and dialogue will be an essential part of that process as they get to know each other better and build mutual trust and understanding. They won't get very far by not talking to one another! But they set off with much common ground between them. And they all shared a common goal.

We all know where we were, what we were doing, on 9/11. Curiously, another 9/11, in another century, marked the beginning of inter-religious dialogue, as we now understand it.

On that day in Chicago in 1893 the World Parliament of Religions was founded. "From now on," declared Charles Bonney, "the great religions of the world will no longer declare war on each other, but on the giant ills that afflict [humankind]."[114] A further conference was convened in 1993 on the centenary of the first, and a series of similar conferences have subsequently come together under the new title 'Parliament of the World's Religions.'

There is a faith line described by the American Indian Muslim Eboo Patel that is no less divisive and no less violent than the 20th century color line of racial segregation that existed after the abolition of slavery.[115] The faith line does not divide different faiths, or separate the religious from the secular. This line is divisive between the values of religious totalitarians, the exclusivists, and the values of the religious pluralists. (Pluralism is not quite the same as inclusivism, which from a Christian perspective takes the view that Christianity is present in all religions, and they are all moving towards Christianity without knowing it. This is an angle not much more conducive to tolerance than exclusivism or totalitarianism!) The totalitarians believe that their way is the only way and are prepared to convert, condemn or indeed kill those who are different, in the name of God. It is this side of the faith line that gives religions a bad press in the eyes of the secular public. The pluralists on the other hand hold that "people believing in different creeds and belonging to different communities need to learn to live together in equal dignity and mutual loyalty." Patel describes pluralism as the belief "that the common good is best served when each community has a chance to make its own unique contribution."[116] Patel founded the Interfaith Youth Core[117] (IFYC) and this serves to promote and support many initiatives between religions, to foster understanding and therefore respect for the long-term.

IFYC has trained thousands of people across continents (Australia, India, Qatar, and across Western Europe for example as well as across America) for the skills needed to transform religious diversity or religious tension into active interfaith cooperation. One way it achieves this is by training college students as leaders to engage with and address topical social issues in an interfaith way, within the college, schools and in the community, wherever there is an identified social need.[118]

We need to build more tolerance between us all, to live and let live, but much more than that, to celebrate and build on our diversities, rather than quarrel about them; because the stakes are now too high, given the deadly weaponry that is available across the world in the hands of those from so many different cultures and creeds.

"We have inherited a big house," said Martin Luther King in his Nobel Peace Prize Lecture in 1964, "a great world house in which we have to live together – black and white, Easterners and Westerners, Gentiles and Jews, Catholics and Protestants, Moslem and Hindu, a family unduly separated in ideas, culture, and interests who, because we can never again live without each other, must learn, somehow, in this one big world, to live with each other."[119]

In his 2005 inauguration sermon Archbishop of York, John Sentamu, urged interfaith dialogue and friendship:

Christians, go and find friends among Buddhists, Hindus, Jews, Muslims, Sikhs, agnostics, atheists – not for the purpose of converting them to your beliefs, but for friendship, under-standing, listening, hearing...

Buddhists, Hindus, Jews, Muslims, Sikhs, agnostics, atheists, go and find friends amongst Christians, not for the purpose of converting them to your beliefs, but for friendship, understanding, listening, hearing.

In other words, seek dialogue.

The classical Greek Athenian philosopher Socrates is credited with inventing dialectic. This is a rigorous discipline designed to expose false beliefs and elicit truth, in a setting of rational discussion that is not dogmatic but encourages courtesy, and consideration for the other's viewpoint. One of the best known sayings of Socrates is "I only know that I know nothing." Too often today, dialogue is aggressive and dogmatic, encouraged, it would seem, by the remote nature of the Internet comment forum, where persons are not face to face, in eye contact, and therefore seem to feel they can rant as much as they like.

But dialogue needs to do better than that. There needs to be genuine dialogue, where there is a real person-to-person relationship, where "each of the participants has in mind the other or others in their particular being and turns to them with the intention of establishing a living mutual relation between himself and them." This is Martin Buber's I/Thou relationship, and contrasts with his I/It relationship where two people do not make that real connection, but treat each other as objects only.[120] In fact dialogue can be even more complicated than that. Some say there may be as many as seven people involved in any dialogue: You and I, my image of you and yours of mine, my image of myself and your image of yourself, where neither of us may be true to who we really are and who the other thinks we are, and finally or indeed first is God – a God of love making the dialogue possible in the first place. Genuine dialogue may be difficult to achieve, but is clearly of great relevance to fostering religious respect and understanding.[121]

With all this in mind, an online dialogue forum has in fact been set up for promoting religious tolerance. It specifically aims "to enable rich and fruitful discussion of scriptural texts between Muslims, Christians and Jews; [to] facilitate deeper under-standing of the lived traditions and beliefs of the three traditions; build trust and friendship between participants; and develop new research methods for collaboratively studying texts across languages."[122] Now that's a splendid and worthy mission. Each piece of text is published in Arab and English, facilitated by a team of professional translators with religious knowledge. To start with, this forum, called Nurani, involved religious leaders, scholars and civic groups, but it ultimately intends to engage the wider public in dialogue. In the fullness of time the site aims to include pages aimed at the media (it is to be hoped that the media will give due weight to the positive in their reporting), and it "will present the thoughtful voices of real religious leaders and scholars on subjects of contemporary interest."

What a brilliant and positive idea this is. Nurani draws on the practice of Scriptural Reasoning,[123] the name given to a dynamic and evolving idea in which Jews, Christians and Muslims meet to study their sacred Scriptures together, often around a common theme. The aim of Scriptural Reasoning is to foster a deeper understanding between the faiths by supporting a process of mutual study, where the participants can listen, question and contribute in a safe environment.

Nurani[124] is part of the Cambridge Inter-Faith Programme, founded in 2002 with a commitment to furthering understanding across the Abrahamic religious traditions. This program is based on the belief that "at the heart of healthy interfaith engagement is a triple dynamic: going deeper into your own faith, deeper into each other's, and deeper into action for the common good of humanity."

Of course there are many other organizations, authors, websites, networks, and by virtue of our wonderful Internet communications all virtually international in their reach, dedicated to fostering and nurturing interfaith dialogue and tolerance, with their own visions for a better future. Religions themselves recognize only too well the need to work with each other, to find effective and lasting ways to bridge the gaps between them.

The academic and comparative study of different religions, as opposed to theology, in schools and universities, gives students the opportunity to visit many different places of worship, witness many different styles of worship by the various faiths, even take advantage of hospitality offered in invitations to mosques and temples and other sacred places that differ from their own experience. Local schools can have special days during the year when they celebrate just one faith that may otherwise be quite unknown to them; our local Christian infant school has an annual day devoted to the celebration of all things Hindu.

Let's pause awhile and think about what we mean by tolerance. If someone is making what I consider to be a huge din next door, playing loud pop 'music' that I find disturbing, I may put up with it or I may bang on the wall between us, ask him to turn it down. I am tolerating his noise, or perhaps not. And that is what tolerance is; putting up with something. But supposing he wasn't really playing his music that loud; just that I prefer Mozart and find that his type of music doesn't speak to me in the same way. How is he to know that? So I go next door and speak with him. Suppose I tried to understand why he enjoys what to me is anathema. Suppose he comes to understand that I am writing, and there are times when I need quiet for concentration and for thinking. And let's suppose that through dialogue we can come to a mutual accommodation. He'll try to turn his music down on the days and times when he knows I am working at my laptop, perhaps close his window. I may never appreciate his musical taste, but I can respect it. I now know that this is his type of release when he gets home from work, an essential part of him 'chilling out'. Of course none of us should have to tolerate antisocial behavior within the norms of society, and neither of us intended to be anti-social! But I've discovered through dialogue that he's not too keen on my bonfires either, because they don't help his asthma. And we have built up a mutual respect through the dialogue we had, because actually now I know him better he's a pleasant guy. I'd been a little nervous about him before we talked, but I've found we do share a passion for growing our own vegetables and for reading books on spirituality! Respect and understanding achieved through dialogue is much more powerful than mere tolerance.

The Dalai Lama once suggested to a multi-faith audience that they should go on pilgrimages with each other, to each other's holy sites. Here they should pray together or at least meditate together, as this, he said, is a very effective way to understand the value and power of other religious traditions.[125]

Gustav Niebuhr, great nephew of Reinhold Niebuhr, calls for an end to what he calls the "rough trade in raw insults"[126] between religions, for example as seen so often on the Internet. He agrees that we need more than mere tolerance; we need a more committed effort to really get to know and respect our religious differences, he writes, to recognize that we can all learn from others, to understand that whatever those differences we are all of equal worth and value across class, race, ethnicity and religion. Respect, a warm acceptance, a mindfulness of everyone's role in society, is called for, akin to the teachings of Gandhi on tolerance, respect and ahimsa.[127]

So on reflection isn't it a just a little demeaning to talk of religious tolerance? Tolerance will never be the full answer. We should be talking in terms of respect, understanding, acceptance and appreciation. Mere tolerance is simply not enough.[128]

And that respect and understanding is only going to come from dialogue between faiths, with the support and cooperation of a responsible media.

There have been four high-profile cases in recent years where the media in both the West and the Middle East have not been helpful in how they have reported the religious issues involved: these were the incidents of the Danish cartoons, the Archbishop of Canterbury Rowan Williams' Shari'a Law lecture, the issue of whether Muslim women in Europe should be permitted to wear headscarves, and Pope Benedict's Regensburg address. In such cases the media tend to:

overdramatize the conflict and to under-research the complex-
ities of lived religious traditions in the modern world... In
each of these cases, with polarizations between blasphemy
and freedom of speech, secular enlightenment and religious
prejudice, it was almost impossible for Westerners to discover
the full range of Islamic (especially Arabic-speaking) views,
with the result that there is a repeated widespread perception
that Muslims are stuck in the Dark Ages. Likewise it was
almost impossible for Arabic speakers to discover the full
range of Western views, with the result that there is a repeated
widespread perception that Europeans are irremediably
decadent and morally corrupt.[129]

Ironically, one of those incidents initiated a response from the
Muslim world that may yet prove to be the most important
catalyst we have yet seen for building greater respect and understanding between the two most powerful and influential world
religions, Islam and Christianity. This is what the world so
desperately needs and has long been crying out for.

The story began in September 2005 when Pope Benedict XVI
gave an address at the University of Regensburg, where he had
once been Professor of Theology, on *Faith, Reason and the
University: Memories and Reflections*. Part of this Regensburg
address, as it became known, was taken as provocative and
insulting by certain parts of the Muslim community, and sparked
mass street protests in many Islamic countries.[130] Pakistan called
on the Pope to retract what it called "this objectionable
statement." The Pope apologized to Muslims and assured them
that the passage quoted did not reflect his own views. Relations
between Muslims and Christians at that time were stormy and
deteriorating. Into this climate a letter was launched, printed in
The New York Times in October 2007, signed by 138 leading
Muslim intellectuals and scholars. It extended a hand to the
leaders of the world's Christian churches and denominations,

including His Holiness Pope Benedict XVI, in a call for peace and harmony between the two religions worldwide. The letter, "A Common Word Between Us and You", outlined the basis of this offering, in the spirit of the shared doctrine of love of God and love of neighbor on which dialogue could be opened.

The handshake was symbolically returned within just over a month, in a letter known as the Yale Response, also published in *The New York Times* (accompanied by the release of an Arabic translation in the United Arab Emirates). It was written originally by four Christian scholars, and then endorsed by more than 500 Christian theologians and leaders, representing many hundreds of millions of Christians across the globe.[131] This exchange of handshakes has produced encouraging results. From these exchanges has grown an organization, based on the expressed purpose to find common ways, in Christianity and Islam, to work together for the social good of all. Grievances are recognized on both sides of the faith divide; it is acknowledged that there are some irreconcilable differences of interpretation on both sides, some difficult questions to deal with. Nonetheless the initiative seems to be making an impact.

Sixty leading Christian figures including H.H. Pope Benedict XVI responded to the document in the two years following its issue. A Common Word has been the subject of major international conferences at Yale University, the University of Cambridge, Lambeth Palace and Georgetown University. By the end of 2011 over 600 Articles had been written about A Common Word in English alone and nearly half a million people had visited its official website.[132] However, while millions will view the latest YouTube frivolity within hours or days, less than 9000 have signed up on the Common Word site since 2007 to endorse its intentions. Now that is sad.

We must all hope that the momentum of this initiative is maintained and that the movement continues to fulfill its promise of ever more understanding and respect between these two great religions.

Relationships between the Muslim and Christian worlds are undoubtedly of the greatest importance in forging a more peaceable future for us all, given the sheer numbers involved, and the grievances, differences, prejudices, and caricatures forged out of misunderstandings, that both religions can claim. Nonetheless, other faiths and belief systems must not be ignored. As Professor David F. Ford, Director of the Cambridge Inter-faith Programme has said:

> Our society is not simply secular; nor is it simply religious; it is both religious and secular in complex ways. If it is to work well there need to be huge numbers of conversations and collaborations across religious and secular boundaries.[133]

From the founding of the World Parliament of Religions in 1893 to the latest A Common Word initiative in 2007 and beyond, has much changed? We have certainly failed to prevent dreadful wars and mass genocides, and we live under greater threats than could have been conceived possible a century ago. We have to continue promoting and forging peaceful dialogue between religions, so that we may come to understand that we are as one in our beliefs to love God and love our neighbor as ourselves. This will need plenty of work by religious leaders, who bear an awesome responsibility for ensuring that this unifying message of love and peace trickles down to the mass population: because trickle down it must! And it will need responsible media. We need their cooperation and support in spreading awareness of the good work being done by religions across the world, in informing the general public of this huge social capital that seems to be largely unappreciated.

As individuals we are not let off the hook either. We have an equally vital role to play: in building on empathy and compassion, and love for all, seeking our own ways of bridging gaps, building up from grass roots. Think of stalactites and stalagmites meeting, of ideas trickling down through the hierarchies, and growing upwards from the masses, until we reach a point of coalescence, where there is a total fusion of ideas and actions, coming from different directions but all working towards the same common good.

But all of this is at what I would regard as the outer level, the exoteric. What about the inner level of experience, the esoteric, the realm of spirituality?

If you are one of those who honestly don't know what is meant by spirituality (and there are some), still stay with me. Because now I shall explore what we mean by spirituality, what are the differences between religion and spirituality, how do they interrelate? Do they overlap, or does one encompass the other? Is spirituality a necessary component of religion and if so why is it not a unifying force between them?

What do current consciousness, mind and brain studies and the exciting new realm of neurotheology tell us about the possibility of a global spiritual awareness? Given that we can steer our own evolution by our actions or inactions, and are conscious that we can do this, how can we steer the world towards a better future? And are there any new philosophies that may help bridge the gap? Some have even suggested a new global religion. Would that help? We need to consider these things, because, as the religious studies scholar and author Ursula King reminds us:

> The spiritual probing of religious pluralism and the drinking from each other's spiritual wells may be today's great spiritual event, full of significance for human well-being, and for the future of humanity on earth.[134]

Chapter 5

Mystics, Meditation and Mind

The most beautiful thing we can experience is the mysterious. It is the source of all true art and science. He to whom this emotion is a stranger, who can no longer pause to wonder and stand wrapped in awe, is as good as dead: his eyes are closed.
Einstein

One of the great tragedies of our age and culture is that so many seem to have thrown the baby out with the bathwater by abandoning religion in favor of scientific 'certainty' (and if you are with me thus far you will understand why I use that word cautiously). Many of the leading philosophers and scientists of our age agree that alongside our scientific achievements we have lost sight of the sacred, the spiritual, and our purpose on the planet; that in spite of the observed increased interest in all matters spiritual, this is not enough. We are in a spiritual crisis as much as a political or ecological one, and this needs urgently addressing.[135]

And without a sense of awe and wonderment at the world around us, without a sense of shared sacredness with our fellow beings, we are capable of the most awful and destructive behavior, a point that is self-evident at this present stage in our evolution.

Both religion and spirituality are such slippery words. Do you think you know the difference? Most of us probably think we know what is meant by religion, but may be less sure about spirituality, and how the two are linked. But I want to show why I think understanding the relationship between the two is important. I also want to explore the possibility that the latest scientific studies into consciousness and other esoteric ideas may somehow give us more clues about a spiritual connectivity, a spirit that brings us all closer together, if we will allow it. Carl Jung had his theory of the "collective unconscious" and wrote of a God Consciousness, an awakening consciousness in the universe.[136] This echoes the higher levels of consciousness recognized within various mystic and meditation practices, and which are generally considered unavailable to the uninitiated, as in the mass population. Perhaps we may find here the links we need to build a greater respect and understanding between all humanity, essential for the future healthy evolution of this planet.

There are so many misunderstandings and misperceptions around what organized religion involves. When people think of religion they often think first about outdated institutions, with strict and inflexible dogma, dry rituals, boring sermons and all the trappings and baggage that go with this image. Then they may conjure up visions of buildings, of mosques and cathedrals, temples and churches (perhaps cold and musty and expensive to maintain!) and synagogues. And many will believe all this to be irrelevant in today's world. Or they may think of some of the worst aspects of religious fundamentalism or of churches operated as highly profitable businesses with flashy buildings and wealthy pastors, that seem to bear little resemblance to the wisdom and teachings of the great mainstream faiths.

My church is nothing like that. The services are very different from those I experienced in my childhood, where I remember those boring sermons, as well as hard pews and gobbledygook language. You can find that in a church near you if you want, but you can also find fellowship, spirituality and community involvement. We have All-Age Family services where we have fun, Taizé services and beautiful music that are spiritually uplifting, children's services, and other alternative styles of worship from time to time to cater for other needs. This for me is far removed from the rigid dogma of which the institutional religions stand accused. And we have exciting workshops for children at Easter and Advent where prayer and worship is combined with the mess and fun of making things, both to take home and to decorate the church. In many churches comfortable chairs replace the old hard pews. There are even easy chairs in house groups, with coffee and home baking laid on! And Christians across the world offer many different styles of Christian worship to suit all tastes: Episcopalian, Anglo-Catholic, Methodist, New Frontiers, Baptist, and so on. So mine is a vibrant church, full of joy and the support of straightforward fellowship, with the sounds and smells of choir and incense, all offered to the glory of God within a traditional style of worship. And the church is where, along with many others, I find my spiritual nourishment. And that is good. That is how it should be.

Traditionally and historically the role of the Christian priest has been the cure of souls and this can be taken to include enhancing people's spiritual growth. Such pastoral care is a healing ministry taken out into the world. And the spiritual care of the soul is common to most if not all of the great faiths.

Unfortunately and maybe even disastrously, the institution-alized structures, leadership roles, rituals and the like that have emerged can lose sight of that basic spiritual remit,[137] buried among the dogma and internal disagreements on issues of the day. At least in part because of that, in many parishes worshippers began to drift away from the Christian church in the second half of the 20th century, so that the church was no longer the center of community life. Some simply felt the entire experience to be irrelevant to their lives, while others thought that they could more honestly follow the teachings of Jesus outside the formal church. The biggest tragedy of all for the church was the way it lost its youngsters as they grew up, and left home and religion behind. Many of these youngsters became the 'spiritual without being religious' group; this still challenges us today. And this is not unique to Christianity. Other religions share the same problem, which needs to be addressed if they are to survive in the long-term.

In spite of this apparent drift away from institutionalized religion, even the most determined 'non-religious' will very often turn to the local church and pastor or other faith leader for support and prayer in times of disaster and grief, for comfort in bereavement and tragedy, perhaps gaining solace from the idea of eternal life. And when I watched those rowing boats set off across the Atlantic from La Gomera, the services of an Anglican priest, ready to bless the boats and the rowers on request, were much in demand. And many who do not regularly attend formal services still want their other rites of passage to happen in the church, their baptisms and marriages, as well as their funerals. Many more come into my own local church to simply sit and pray and meditate and cry and light candles. What is that about?

But this book is not intended to be about Christian mission, although for all the reasons I have shown I believe it to be hugely important that religion does survive. There are good up to date books available that are unashamedly missiological.[138] I am concerned here with the survival of all religion, and with promoting respect and understanding between different religious and spiritual traditions, and thinking about how we do this. And I think that respect needs to start at grass root level, with the local religious groups. If there is poor understanding and little deference here it will surely be very difficult to nurture a wider respect beyond our own small circle of existence.

So what is spirituality? What do you and I mean by the word. Words and phrases such as 'search for meaning and purpose,' 'filling a void' in our hearts or lives, the transcendent, soul, consciousness and interconnectedness of all beings, the numinous, divinity, God, inner peace, and perhaps many others will variously spring to mind. So spirituality is used in a vast range of contexts and there are perhaps as many attempts at a definition as there are spiritual writers, and different cultures and religions.[139] Perhaps it cannot be defined. Perhaps we do not need a definition that is 'all things to all men.' The mystics of different religious traditions, the Muslim Sufi for example, the Christian mystics, or the Jewish Kabbalah probably get closest to articulating their spiritual experiences. But we don't have to be mystics and monks to find spiritual experience. It is found within all the established religions and wisdom traditions, which not only provide a rich supply of spiritual experiences, they can and do play a part in nurturing and kindling spirituality. Sadly there are many among us who fail to appreciate that organized religion can and does satisfy this need, can and does help us grow spiritually without recourse to the expensive trappings of commerce. The danger comes when spirituality becomes wrapped in those commercial trappings, with the promise of peace of mind, spiritual growth, wealth and success and happiness: but at a price. Even 'care of the psyche' in current psychotherapy language sounds very like 'cure of the soul' to me! And in seeking a secular definition of spirituality a transcendent dimension often seems to creep in, that may "include the traditional view of a personal God"(!)[140]

Although not everyone can relate to the idea of spirituality, we are all intrinsically spiritual beings, and one only has to look around us, in our media, in the mind/body/spirit sections of our bookshops, in our shopping malls and main streets, in our art galleries and concert halls to notice the significant role that spirituality plays in many lives. Even atheists can acknowledge the 'spiritual' experience they feel at the awe and wonder of nature, or when 'lost' in a sublime work of art or music.

As people drifted away from the traditional institutionalized religions many found that the New Age spiritualities came in to fill the spiritual vacuum in their lives. The Age of Aquarius brought in a new concept of spirituality, distinct from traditional religions. It seems that the sheer scale of current interest in all kinds of spirituality harks back to that need that religion no longer fulfills in the minds of many. But herein lies danger, because all kinds of contemporary notions of spirituality appeared. Sadly this has also spawned charlatans with wacky ideas, many motivated far more by business greed and the trappings of commercialism than a genuine desire to nurture spirituality. These New Age spiritualities have been castigated as "bespoke metaphysical marshmallow... non-specific, unlocated, thin, uncritical, dull and un-nutritious,"[141] and furthermore these may have little to do with the Christian (or indeed any other religion's) tradition of Spirit and spirituality, which is "altogether more uncomfortable, astringent, challenging and *world-focussed*." The italics are mine. So much 'spirituality' seems to exist mainly to feed the self-centered Me-Millennium attitude, to make us feel better inside purely for our own satisfaction. That is not my kind of spirituality.

So does spirituality have its roots in religion? Or is religion a subsection of a vaster overarching spirituality?[142] Some claim the human phenomenon of spirituality to be more basic, to have preceded religion. But religion itself is very old. This raises confusion again as to how they are linked. It seems like a chicken and egg situation. But it does seem probable that religion developed to meet man's earliest spiritual need. This makes sense if we think of religion as being there first and foremost to nourish spiritual growth. And I use the male term deliberately; since it was relatively recently in humanity's history that woman was generally deemed to be capable of spiritual experience. Indeed even now her religious and spiritual needs and expressions are marginalized in some cultures. Thus spirituality may be seen as the more general term, including religion, and being a core aspect of religion. Although this does not deny that there are 'spiritual but not religious' individuals or that extrinsically religious people may not be especially 'spiritual.'

So we see that the relationship between religion and spirituality is far from cut and dried and to some extent it is controversial. Spirituality is a rapidly developing subject for academic study in many universities and there is a vast growth in literature, and conferences to explore the issues and to encourage dialogue about spirituality with different faiths.[143]

I have thought a great deal about this and am persuaded that true spirituality and religion are so closely associated that they cannot be truly separated. Whatever we think we mean by both phenomena, it is probably unhelpful to separate them too sharply, at least at this stage in our level of understanding.[144] I am inclined to agree with the view that "the two have a kind of symbiotic relationship as, in a sense, two complementary forms of social presentation of what is ultimately a single phenomenon."[145] In other words I agree with the idea that spirituality is "the way we hold the what of our faith"[146] and that spiritual care is best coming from within religious tradition and cannot be generic. Indeed, generic spirituality has been dubbed a kind of "spiritual Esperanto" in an essay called "Dumbing Down the Spirit," by the pastoral theologian Stephen Pattison.[147] He warns that the ability of the religious traditions to contribute to the current search for spirituality is being weakened by this more generalized spiritual quest.[148] This is good enough reason for the religions to change, and fast!

How do we address our spiritual crisis and recover our souls? Ursula King writes that the solution is to be found in our rich heritage of the world's spiritualities. If we link spirituality in any way with religion (and how can we not?) then this quest also has to be extended to our rich heritage of the world's religions. They can help, they must help, and they are helping in this journey of rediscovery!! Therefore don't throw out the baby with the bathwater, the religion with the dogma! We need religions! This is unlikely to please those who proudly proclaim that they are spiritual but not religious. I believe there is an urgent need for religions to redefine their role, to embrace the spiritual more obviously and more openly: for religion to return more fully to its spiritual roots. And to let the world know, through a sympathetic media, that this is happening!

I also believe there is great potential for finding common ground between all spiritualities, all religions, all people in the quest for something beyond definition, perhaps what some may mean by the Holy Spirit, or the Transcendent, a true spiritual oneness of humanity, a global spiritual interdependence available to everyone, whether or not we believe in God the Creator of all things visible and invisible.

Will this help us address our religious intolerances and divides? I think it could. If we can truly promote a global spiritual awakening this gives us great hope for human flour-ishing.[149] How do we do this?

With the death of the Reverend Professor John Hick in 2012, at the age of 90, we lost one of our greatest and most influential philosophers of religion. His pluralist approach proved provocative, particularly among Christian fundamentalists in the States, where over the years he held several teaching posts. He believed in an ultimate ineffable Real (his generic term for Transcendent Reality), whose universal presence could be felt in a variety of ways, making sense of the variety of forms of religion that have developed around the world. He held that Truth claims about God are really Truth claims about our individual percep-tions of God, affected by specific cultures and histories, leading to the claims made by different religions, none of which can therefore claim to know the Absolute Truth.[150]

It seems to be such a blindingly obvious idea, but isn't it just possible that when we have our spiritual experiences we are all tapping into the same spirit, higher level of consciousness, transcendence, whatever we may choose to call it, even the Holy Spirit? Why then can we not use this spirituality as the common thread that binds and unites all religions? Because, after all, this indefinable global consciousness, soul, spirit, empathy is presumably of the same character whether we are Christian,

Muslim, Jains, atheists, agnostics, black, white, Scottish or Zulu or whatever our faith, color or culture.

I've mentioned the workshops our church holds for our young children at Advent and Good Friday, where they have a great deal of fun before they all go over to the church across the road for a very short service. In order to cross the road safely and so that no children stray, they all hold on to a long rope until their journey is completed safely. I've seen parties of school children using the same device. The rope could be a metaphor for that elusive spiritual common denominator between all people, between different races and creeds, something that binds us all together at a profound inner level while allowing our differences in all their fullness, uniqueness and divinity.

The original great teachers of spiritual Truth didn't set out to create highly organized and institutionalized religions, continually at loggerheads with one another, creating power struggles between their own sacred empires. No indeed. If they had all come together to formulate the one true religion/spirituality, what would they all have in common? Accomplished musician, lecturer, writer, educator and workshop leader first in the USA and now England, James D'Angelo, has suggested a consensus of characteristics.[151] Briefly, we all have a spirit or soul, he proposes, which has eternal life, as there is no death at this level of being. If we can accept that premise, then we should have a deep compassion and love for all other souls or spirits, for all other mortal beings. We call that feeling love. There would be continual reincarnation until we cease to be enmeshed in the material world, and the first objective of life should be non-attachment. The second objective would be to inherit eternal life. D'Angelo goes on to say that our material world is staining our souls, and that the ignorance of the Truth that we display is in Christian terms what we mean by sin. Now I don't wish to be branded a heretic, doomed to eternal hell and damnation. But I do think that some at least of these ideas meld well with my own

Christian religious beliefs.

In the light of these precepts, D'Angelo believes that the primary work of religions should be the care of souls, and I certainly agree with that. Indeed I would broaden the scope to include the healing of souls. I think D'Angelo is making some important points. Here surely is the link between the religions. Some seem to demonstrate and practice this care and cure of souls better than others. We approach it in our Taizé services. We can all approach it in meditation and prayer if we are given the right conditions. It is not easy to achieve in the noise and busyness of some church services. While sermons and homilies advance our understanding and help us grow in our faith, they do not always touch any spiritual chord, unless we have an exceptional pastor.

And this is where reform is needed in our religions, certainly within the Christian church. Religions are missing a vital trick if they are not prepared to learn lessons from the drift towards the New Age style of spirituality and to address the spiritual needs of the 21st century. They need to change to become once again the main and true providers of spiritual nourishment and growth, to steer their flocks away from dangerous false spirituality. They also need to address science head on and be in no doubt in their teachings as to the compatibility of science with religion, to give their followers the confidence and tools to take religion out into the world, into life and the workplace, to gain wide respect again, while of course remaining true to their own faiths, in my case the Christian gospel message.

And the Christian church clearly needs to change its image and its processes. There is an urgent need to stop its internal bickering around gender and sexuality issues. It needs to practice tolerance within its own faith, put its own house in order. There needs to be a move away from hard evangelism towards a different kind of mission: reaching out to those in need in the way Jesus taught us. Because congregations can and do flourish when the formula is right, as we have demonstrated locally and in our cathedral congregations.

Charles Foster even goes so far as to say we should abandon the description 'Christian.' We've wrecked the word, he says. It has negative connotations of anti-gay, hypocritical, judgmental. How about Jesus Wanderer, or Jesus Follower, he suggests.[152] Would that catch on? I wonder.

If the churches would only change and go back to these roots, they could help the esoteric needs of the world as effectively as they now help the exoteric. Because here we have social capital writ large, that we need to save.

Many people seem very pessimistic about religion and whether it has the capacity or ability to reform. I see hope in organizations such as Christians Awakening to a New Awareness, or CANA, and the World Community for Christian Meditation, or WCCM, the latter founded in the early 1990s and now with 2000 meditation groups in 114 countries.[153] I find the inclusive open-mindedness of some churches encouraging.[154] I find hope in the meditational and reflective quiet evenings that my local churches are beginning to organize. These are all examples of Christians exploring their faith in a more spiritual setting away from dogma and doctrine, communities of explorers who have Christian roots and share different experiences and insights for living out the teachings of Jesus in holistic and integrated ways.

I went to a Christian conference where we explored how we could best use in our churches the many new digital media opportunities available to us. And right at the beginning we were told to switch on our smart phones and laptops. Yes, we really were told to switch them on, not off! And all through the day there was a continual twitter roll, moving relentlessly across the screens at each side of the main lecture hall, full of a constant chatter of tweets from the assembled 360 delegates. How distracting was that!! And isn't it somehow rude? Not listening with full attention to the words of wisdom from the platform? Even if the tweets are comments on what the speaker has just said? Perhaps I'm just old-fashioned! The delegates obviously all felt very connected by all this. But surely this connection can only be at an exoteric level?

I felt very 'disturbed' at a heart and soul level by this digital 'noise.'

I attend quite a few conferences in the course of my research and in following my fairly eclectic interests. And I have to say that I find the clicking of laptop keyboards all around me incredibly distracting as people take notes: not to mention the flashes of mobiles as they take photos of the PowerPoint presentations. Doesn't this distract the speakers? It all seems a long way away from my student days when all we had were pencils and lined notepads and we scribbled furiously to get everything down before the lecturer moved on to the next topic.

Apparently the University of Carolina jams technology in the lecture theatre to eliminate distractions away from the important matter in hand, the lecture itself. And I suspect many other educational institutions are beginning to do the same thing.

I tell these stories to make a serious point. There is quite simply too much noise!

Some say the Internet, even Twitter, is providing a spiritual network, perhaps along the lines of the vision of Teilhard de Chardin, when he wrote of the Noosphere, the Omega Point and a coalescence of consciousness.[155] Certainly there are now plenty of networks on the Internet that by name are spiritual. But that is what they are: just names and spiritless networks. I think these simply connect the outer spiritual beings, people with an interest in the spiritual. They cannot evoke the spiritual experience itself, the inner experience. I don't think the ceaseless digital and exoteric inconsequential chatter and noise of Twitter and Tweets, or Facebook, is at the right consciousness or spiritual level for true healing of the world, for providing a common spiritual denominator that will bind the many different beliefs and experiences together in true harmony and respect. I don't believe that the coalescence of consciousness of which de Chardin spoke is being fulfilled in this way. That is not where humanity will be healed, where total mutual respect and understanding will be born. Teilhard de Chardin spoke of bringing together our hearts, not our heads or bodies. Constant electronic noise, however much it is used to make connections between humans, distracts from our inner spiritual being, from our spiritual connectivity. It is true that in that conference I mentioned we were shown many wonderful opportunities that digital media could bring to our churches, helping people to connect with what was going on. But that sense of spiritual togetherness, of love and harmony between all sentient beings, is found in group meditation, prayer, worship, and in the sound of silence, not in digital noise. The experience of meditating in a group of fifty or more like-minded souls in a large conference hall or lecture theatre is far more powerful, nurturing and interconnecting than any Internet network or Twitter storm. And I believe that it may well be our increasing understanding of the mysteries of our global human consciousness, as it relates to our spirituality, and not digital connections, which will finally bring humans together to live and work in peaceful love and compassion and cooperation regardless of color or faith or creed.

And scientific research is bringing us that greater understanding, perhaps even closing some of the gap between science and religion.

Chapter 6

New Wisdom and New Ideas

"That's a question for a neurotheologian."
"Meaning what?" he asked.
"Meaning precisely what it says. Somebody who thinks about people in terms, simultaneously, of the Clear Light of the Void and the Vegetative Nervous System."
Aldous Huxley, *Island*, 1962

Dean Radin[156] was brought up within an artistic family and wanted to be a concert violinist; so as a youngster he clocked up something like 10,000 hours of violin practice. And he is convinced that this early background encouraged his sense of the supernatural. Great art, in this case the sublime sound of the violin skillfully played, puts us in touch, as very few things can, with the spirit within us, perhaps even with our soul. So Radin changed his career path and became a highly trained scientist, in the fields of mathematics, physics and engineering.

Radin has become known for his pioneering work into the study of consciousness and in particular its ability to extend beyond the individual brain and body to envelop people at a distance, even outside the present moment. Of course the conventional view is that consciousness, whatever we understand by it, is confined to the individual, and dies with us, and Radin's ideas seem crazy to many. But there is plenty of scientific evidence, including a huge database going back decades, collected under controlled conditions and published in peer-reviewed scientific journals, supporting the human ability to convey information to other people at a distance, and also to acquire information from people at a distance and outside the present moment.

The American physician Larry Dossey is known for his work on spiritual healing. He has been Executive Editor of the peer-reviewed journal *Alternative Therapies in Health and Medicine* and insists in his work on scientific legitimacy, with an equally insistent focus on "what the data show." He has lectured all over the world, including at major medical schools and hospitals in the United States.[157]

Dossey's work gives evidence for the idea that the mind is unconfined to the brain and body, and "can be spread infinitely throughout space and time," a concept introduced in his 1989 book *Recovering the Soul*.[158] Dossey, along with experts in Near Death Experiences such as psychologist and medical doctor Raymond Moody (who coined the phrase) and neuropsychiatrist Peter Fenwick, believe on evidence that consciousness does survive death. Dossey calls this consciousness 'non-local' and demonstrates it in non-local healing phenomena that "appear almost always to involve consciousness: the empathic, loving intent of one individual to help another."[159] The Institute of Noetic Sciences has conducted its own studies on distance healing and the relationship between consciousness and healing.[160]

We call these happenings psychic or psi phenomena. And these ideas are all coming from highly educated, highly intelligent and highly trained scientists.

There are clearly links between us at some deep level in our consciousness otherwise psychic phenomena such as Near Death Experiences and distance healing would not be possible. But they are real; they do exist.

If there is so much scientific evidence for this idea of extended consciousness why are so many people so skeptical and why are so few scientists engaged in research in this field?

Put bluntly, it is because this would be a bad career move! Science has its own ideas about what is publicly acceptable, and highly controversial topics attract the least funding. It's really that simple. (Scientist Rupert Sheldrake did nothing for his own academic career at the time when he propounded his own theories of morphic resonance, although he's certainly made up for it since!) For much the same reason, unexpected or supposedly 'inexplicable' experimental results can be suppressed and never published. Few scientists can afford to put their livelihood on the line by going 'outside the box' in their research.

Of course, as Radin himself admits, there is ample scope for scholarly debate about these topics, and not every informed scientist is going to reach the same conclusions. But, he writes, "I've also learned that those who assert with great confidence that there isn't any scientifically valid evidence for psychic abilities just don't know what they're talking about. In addition, the rants one finds in various online 'skeptical' forums appear to be motivated by fundamentalist beliefs of the scientistic or religious kind, and not by a rational assessment of the relevant literature."

Yes indeed. I also want to go 'outside the box'. Not only do I think it highly likely that such scientific studies are getting very close to discovering our soul, and the idea of there being life after death; I also find them broadly compatible with the thoughts of the great mystics, and with many of my own beliefs within the Christian faith.

Let's take the subject of prayer. The new atheists love to mock anything that they see as pseudo science and a favorite target is intercessory prayer, or praying for other people. Dawkins specifically sneers at what he calls The Great Prayer Experiment.[161] This took place in 2005/2006 in various American hospitals, among 1802 heart patients, who were either prayed or not prayed for, who knew or didn't know about the experiment, and where the usual blind/double blind controls were set up. Dawkins gloats that this didn't give, as he says, the result the

Christians wanted! This he takes as yet more proof that there is no God.

Some critics would say that it is hard to see that prayer produced for such an experiment could be genuine, and God is hardly likely to view with favor his people testing His ability to answer prayer. Of course Dawkins would say that we would say that!

In fact prayer experiments go back quite a way. In 1988 Byrd, a devout Christian and a cardiologist at the San Francisco General Hospital, was struck by a conversation with a colleague about a terminally ill cancer patient. All medical avenues had been exhausted and the physicians really did not know what else they could do for the patient. We could try prayer, said Byrd.[162] Thus began the prayer study that has inspired so many subsequent experiments into non-local healing phenomena. The scientifically designed and double blind trials produced more positive responses in those groups of patients who were prayed for, when compared with the control groups. Yes the sample was small and the statistical interpretation of the results controversial, but Byrd's work was a catalyst for physicians such as Larry Dossey who was interested in exploring the spiritual questions of medicine within wider parameters beyond the known interaction of mind and body. And this set a whole train of experiments in motion. So much so that there is now a very considerable body of research that, when it is all brought together into what we as scientists call a meta analysis of the data, shows overall the considerable positive contribution that Christianity and other religion makes to the well-being of its followers: higher self-esteem, happiness, life satisfaction, less anxiety, less substance abuse, more children, and so on.[163]

But Dawkins and the new atheists generally would rather not know about that!

The initial knee-jerk reaction of many to advances in scientific knowledge was to abandon religion as being irrelevant to humanity that now thought it knew better. But, as I have already indicated, there is increasing support for the belief that science and religion can no longer be regarded as totally incompatible. There have also been exciting developments in research into the connections between mind and brain and religious or spiritual experiences. Not surprisingly much of the current research in such areas comes from the medical world as here there is easier access to the laboratory facilities, especially the brain scanning technology that is so often a part of the work, as well as a ready supply of patients to volunteer for the experiments!

Empirical and scientifically measurable studies on spiritual tools such as intuition, dreams and stories of coincidence, alongside prayer studies, provide a sound foundation for those who believe that medicine can be imbued in some way with spirit.

Of course it is understandable that many may be skeptical about prayer experiments on human beings. Quite apart from objections already raised above, they may point out, quite justifiably, that the results can be affected by the subjects' own positive thinking, or by them praying for themselves, for example. So in response to the critics Dossey used mice, yeast cells, barley seeds and human tissue cultures in his experiments, to eliminate such bias. In his book *Reinventing Medicine* (2000) he relates stories of such experiments, devised to see if prayer or other healing intention had any effect on the subjects chosen. As far as possible he used conditions and analyses as stringent as any employed in traditional drug trials. In one such experiment, for example, mice were measured for their ability to heal from a deliberate wound made on their backs. The subjects were divided into three groups. The group that was exposed to the attentions of a healer showed a statistically significant healing rate above that of the group looked after by inexperienced medical students with no interest in healing, or by the control group. Similarly, it has been shown that yeast cells respond with an increased growth rate to the attentions of spiritual healers when compared with the attention of those disinterested students. It has to be assumed that mice and yeast cells are incapable of imposing their own bias to the experiments!

Inspired by his belief in faith's healing power, and by personal experience Harold G. Koenig[164] has spent many years studying the impact of people's religious life on their physical and emotional health. He shows how prayer can very definitely help people come through serious afflictions and improve the outcome of many illnesses. He relates many such stories of hope and inspiration in *The Healing Power of Faith*,[165] which he later followed up with *The Healing Connection: The Story of a Physician's Search for the Link Between Faith and Health.*[166]

Are all these studies bringing explanations to what humankind has known intuitively throughout his time on earth? That we are spiritual beings first and foremost, with empathic and spiritual interconnectivity at the level of consciousness? But we are allowing these wonderful possibilities to be crowded out by the superficial, the inane and the trivial in our lives. Facebook may be a valuable tool for human connectivity at an exoteric level, but it cannot surely provide any meaningful substitute for the esoteric spiritual experiences, within our "deeper level of consciousness," perhaps at the level of the Holy Spirit?[167]

Now we have the whole new discipline of neurotheology, first envisaged by Aldous Huxley as a philosophical construct, in his novel *Island*.

Neurotheology, sometimes called spiritual neuroscience, is the scientific attempt to correlate neural phenomena in the brain with subjective spiritual experiences. Is there a neurological and evolutionary basis for the spiritual and the religious? Dr. Andrew Newberg is a pioneer in this research. In his work, which has included brain scans of people in prayer, meditation, rituals, and various trance states, he has shown that spiritual experiences involve a neurological process, which can be traced through brain activity. This of course could lead to a conclusion that God is 'all in the mind'. But Newberg is quite clear from his own rigorously conducted scientific experiments that spiritual experiences are not "in any way less real to the brain than any other information it receives and processes, including perceptions of the material world and everyday life."[168] We cannot, he rightly claims, trust one without trusting the other.

Work of doctors such as Dossey and Koenig who are recognizing a further healing dimension in medicine beyond the body and brain, and the ideas of the scientists such as Radin and Newberg are, I believe, incredibly important in helping us gain an understanding of a further dimension in religion beyond the dogma and doctrine. There is a massive overlap between the phenomena described by the scientists and the power of prayer, meditation and healing for example in a religious or spiritual setting. But there is still a great deal of prejudice against these views, particularly those where the focus is specifically on religion, rather than on a more generalized concept of spirituality.

Why does all this matter in the current context? Firstly and perhaps most obviously, I believe that we need to build a society where religion can come out of the closet and be respected for what it is. And this applies in all areas of our life, 24/7.

But I also think that all these ideas have a deeper significance for religious tolerance. Because there seems to be the potential for so much common ground between the findings of scientists and doctors such as Newberg, Byrd, Dossey and Koenig and the spirit and power of prayer, meditation and spirituality in any religious setting, whatever our faith or religion or creed. These phenomena all seem to provide explanations in various ways for some of our religious beliefs and experiences. Eternal life, prayer and meditation, distance healing: latest science is surely lending support to such beliefs, not destroying them?

It would be extreme to say that religions need reinvention,

but they certainly need to change, to adapt to a changing world. They need to return to their spiritual roots, to learn again how to cater for our spiritual needs. But perhaps they also need to bridge the gap with science, be receptive to what latest science is showing us. Perhaps we can begin to understand religions better through the latest consciousness studies; religions should possibly no longer ignore the evidence for many supernatural phenomena, such as out of body experiences, non-local healing, and so on. Maybe they need to tap into what many who call themselves spiritual but non-religious intuitively know already: we are all interconnected at some level of consciousness or spirit or energy level.

Are we on the cusp of recognizing with new eyes the link that has always been there but has been lost in the digital noise of the last few decades? Perhaps it will be such a link that in the end will help to bind all religions, faiths and spiritual philosophies together, help us all understand and respect each other, feel a deep mutual empathy, without in any way destroying the basic tenets of each faith? Newberg is attracted very much to this possibility. So am I.

As Proust observed, "The real voyage of discovery consists not in seeking new landscapes but in having new eyes."

New philosophies for a new world

Philosophers will always want to challenge the status quo with new and sometimes exciting ideas, and creative thinking is going to be at its most astute and best when we seem under threat from forces that stretch our understanding, that are beyond our comfort zones. And if the threat is serious, that is when humanity is steered most towards cooperative behavior and away from competition. I hope that sooner rather than later enough people on this earth will truly take on board the enormity of the task ahead of us, that a sufficient critical mass will be achieved, to make a real difference to the way we live; so that all humanity, 7 billion now and rising, will have access to adequate food, water, healthcare, education, and justice for all. Could that happy state of affairs be in sight, with the help of the enormous strength of the world's religions and with the genuine spirituality that they nurture, that could connect all people? Remember the awesome scale of religion across the world, which no amount of atheist campaigning is going to dent.

Let's start with Stuart Kauffman, American theoretical biologist and bio-complexity expert, calling for a new scientific worldview of God in *Reinventing the Sacred*.

He proposes that we are all members of a natural universe of "ceaseless creativity, in which life, agency, meaning, value, consciousness and the full richness of human action have emerged." He describes this concept as awesome, stunning and worthy of reverence, something we can all view as sacred. He believes, from the evidence of the origins of life in the universe, that we do not need a creator God. (But what about the origin of the universe itself?) Instead he calls for one global view of a common God as being the natural creativity itself in the universe. Kauffman's vision is that by harnessing our personal and collective responsibilities we have the wisdom, ability and knowledge to develop a new global ethics, and steer our evolution forwards through his proposed 'reinvention' of the sacred.

Kauffman describes four injuries of the modern world: the artificial division between the sciences and humanities; the need for more value and meaning in our lives; the need for spirituality for all, atheists, humanists, agnostics as well as those of faith; and finally the need for a global ethic. He believes that his ideas, based as they are on a broader scientific worldview than current conventional science, may provide a shared religious and spiritual space for us all, within which he hopes we can heal those injuries.

Kaufman offers ideas for a future evolution steered by us for a safer and better global place to live, aiming to address the schism between faith and reason, between science and arts, between reason and other sensibilities, in a new way; it is time, he writes, to "heal the split," for the sake of our world. He is absolutely right. But he can also be controversial and provocative, and as a Christian who believes in an Abrahamic Creator God I cannot agree with all he writes (although perhaps I have already been labeled a heretic!) But it's a jolly good idea nonetheless! And I have a respect for his beliefs.

The Polish Philosopher Henryk Skolimowski seeks different answers to the increasingly urgent call for a new worldview, for a revival of spirituality and transcendence, in another inspiring book *Let There be Light*.

Skolimowski's philosophy is of cosmic creativity and evolution and light that unite us all as the source of all life. To understand the cosmos and its evolution and the part we play we must understand the nature of light, and its evolutionary role along the path to enlightenment. Skolimowski thinks of traditional religions and science as both having filters. In religion these prevent us experiencing the full spiritual transcendence needed for this world. Science also has its filters, becoming totally reductionist, and its rationality has become limiting and crippling. It has used Darwinian evolution as a hatchet against religion, but has never tried to understand religion and finds it hard to accept that there can be any theories of evolution beyond Darwin. And physics, he argues, makes preposterously arrogant assumptions about the laws of life. And he sees profanity in modern science and technology. He calls this "mistletoe technology," which he says is strangling the whole tree of life.

He believes that we are in the midst of a gigantic struggle between the old mechanistic consciousness and a new spiritually inclined consciousness, and the latter needs to assert itself. We have come to the point where we must choose madness or sanctity, and we have only been saved so far from madness by the great and beautiful art and music and literature, sacred and otherwise that is available to us. But much of our art is now ugly; perpetuating the ugliness we have created around us. And ugliness is carcinogenic. Without beauty we wither. Artists therefore have a responsibility in this. "We can and must re-articulate human nature," Skolimowski writes, "away from the ugly and destructive; and towards beautiful, transcendent and noble." Furthermore, "the violence done to beauty has been violence done to our souls and lives... the loss of spirituality is one of the consequences."[169]

We need wisdom, and an essential task before us is to nurture the seed of the spirit and the divine. Skolimowski therefore proposes meditational practices of mind and body and light, to nurture our spiritual being. It is clear there is much wrong with our present social contract, and the need to design a new one is urgent. But this needs a leap of transcendence, which must be spiritual. Religions, he says, need a renewal at source. And unless we rise to that challenge to change ourselves, politicians and political scientists will continue in their old ways and the world will not heal. Because they will not change by themselves, conditioned as they are by the past and possessed by the "collective un-wisdom of our time... The institutions only reflect who you are, including your indolence and lack of responsibility." Skolimowski sets an important challenge for us all.

Modern mystic and visionary Andrew Harvey comes from a different direction with his ideas on psychic free radicals of collective unconscious, which he claims are penetrating our individual psychic fields. This clearly has some common features with some of what was said above about scientific studies on consciousness and psi. His book *Sacred Activism* is a call to bring consciousness of the sacred into everything we do, to be agents of profound change. Harvey lectures on his idea and has founded his Institute of Sacred Activism, from which he is setting up Networks of Grace and a Global Curriculum, extolling the virtues of his own particular brand of Divine Transformative Power and evolutionary mysticism.[170]

Harvey shows a respect for the faiths and religious beliefs held by others, for the wisdom of elders and his love for Jesus Christ, the greatest love of his heart throughout his life, he claims. But this is the Jesus Christ of the Gospel of Thomas, and many may be unable to reconcile the Gnostic teachings of Christ with their own faith.

Nonetheless, "hope for our survival lies in massive spiritual transformation and radical action," he writes, and I cannot disagree with that, although the reader will by now understand that I think this should be the domain of the established religions. After many years of study and immersing himself in different mystical traditions and their sacred texts, which he uses generously throughout his book, Harvey forms a vision of a new mystic spirituality. It is hard to disagree with the aims of any mysticism that calls for love and compassion in all we do, for unconditional forgiveness, and that understands our innate need to live in joy and peace, with total respect and love for all sentient beings. But this is the message of Jesus Christ. We don't need another religion based on His teachings!

The problem I have with Harvey and his Institute of Sacred Activism is that his ideas are already put into practice in churches everywhere; the prayer, bible study, Lent and other church based groups I attend seem very similar to his Networks of Grace by another name. In fact I am not sure that the world needs another spirituality or mysticism when most of his ideas can be found, albeit perhaps expressed differently, across all the great faiths, in the teachings of the mystics and in ancient wisdom, as he will know from his own spiritual explorations.

I am always interested in books that call for urgent change in our troubled world and particularly if the proposals support practical actions that are accessible to us all and are spiritually based in the very best sense of the word. But let me again offer a word of warning. It seems that we have an insatiable appetite for uncritically checking into the latest spiritual ideas, and do not seem to mind how much we spend in the process! Take care. There are business enterprises built around the spiritual wisdoms already taught and nurtured by the great religions, put within a different wrapper to market anew! And the cynic in me suggests that some of these ideas may be simply money- making devices. As such, they remind me of the worst aspects of some of the religious 'sects' that can suck the unwary into their folds and cause untold havoc to sensitive souls.[171]

How many more new ideas will emerge from so many before we realize that what we already have is actually all we need:

Our ancient religions, our faiths and our spirituality?

Empathy and compassion

To the shame of all the established religions, it has taken a secular initiative to kick-start what the world desperately needs and what those religions all teach through the Golden Rule; that we should all be loving our neighbors as ourselves, showing compassion for all.

The religions' historian Karen Armstrong was frustrated that not enough was seemingly being done by the world's religions to promote their own moral codes of love and compassion. Perhaps this was a fair indictment. Compassion manifests itself in the world, she says, not by thinking but by doing and she wants to bring compassion back to the very heart of moral and spiritual life.[172] So with the support of the Fetzer Institute[173] and a multi-faith, multi-national council of thinkers and leaders who helped with the drafting, the Charter for Compassion was launched globally in 2009.[174] It is an idea whose time had definitely come.

Compassion literally means 'to suffer with or alongside' someone. We identify with you in your suffering; we can show mercy or sorrow with you in your pain. Empathy goes a little further and is the capacity to experience what it is like to be someone else. We can bare our own souls and walk in your shoes to share your suffering. That is true empathy, although the two words are often used interchangeably. Scientifically empathy should not be possible, but it is! It is different from and goes way beyond sympathy or pity, and requires well-developed imagination, "the great instrument of moral good."[175]

There is an emerging science of empathy that is demonstrating that we are actually wired for empathy and compassion, that empathy exists at a neurophysiological level and that we are not just the outcome of a selfish gene. We all have the natural potential for showing empathy or concern to others, and this can be nurtured or crushed by the circumstances of our upbringing. But we need that affection from birth. The development of our mind depends on interactions face to face. Neuroscience tells us that specific brain areas respond to kindness and compassion and there is a correlation between the size of a child's brain and the attention or neglect he experiences. Children who have not received sufficient care and compassion can feel unlovable, and can be high in self-criticism. In other words our social and developmental psychology is affected by the way we are brought up. This of course gives us a totally different understanding of human nature and has enormous significance for our societies. While our religion might teach us to be compassionate and loving, our upbringing might very well take us away from the possibility of such behavior coming naturally to us. It then needs to be re-learned, nurtured and encouraged. And it should be the religions that are there to bring us back on track.

In the 'outer' world of our experience, a term I am using to distinguish from the spiritual experience of empathy itself, there is plenty of resource building up on the Internet in networks and e-zines.

The Center for Building a Culture of Empathy is probably the largest Internet portal for resources and information about the values of empathy and compassion, with articles, conferences, definitions, experts, history, interviews, videos, science and much more.[176]

But at the 'inner' esoteric level of our experience I can see this great push towards building empathy and compassion as another spiritual thread that can bind us all regardless of color or creed; an underlying web of interconnectedness and interdependence, linking human beings and perhaps the whole of creation at an emotional level. This has been called empathetic resonance.[177] Perhaps we could also think of this as resonance between individual souls?

Here is an urgent call for us all to foster both spirituality and compassion, with a hefty dose of ancient wisdom, before the seemingly insatiable Western appetite for soulless materialism, consumerism and unsustainable economic growth takes over and destroys humanity.

Time for transformational spirituality

Former Jain monk Satish Kumar was just nine when he left his family home to join the wandering Indian religious order. Nine years later he decided that he could achieve more out in the world. He has been a peace and environment activist ever since, "quietly setting the Global Agenda for change for over 50 years."[178]

Ursula King, in her book *The Search for Spirituality*, explains the two models of spirituality seen within the great religious traditions through the ages. First is the ascetic or monastic model, where spiritual growth and perfection is sought through physical separation from the world at large. We see this in the Christian and Buddhist Communities of monks and nuns. Then there is the transformative, ethical, responsible spirituality I have called for elsewhere, infusing everything we do, which she calls "householder spirituality." This is a "spirituality of living in the world," of relating it to our whole lives, that she describes as more socially involved, more ethically engaged and certainly most needed today. Such a "householder," she writes, will differ little from other people, "but inner attitudes and outer actions are transformed by the adherence to spiritual teachings and disciplines that can be practiced in the setting of daily work and family commitments."[179] And this has to be at three levels, the personal, the local and the global, ultimately renewing the earth, in Thomas Berry's words, as a "biospiritual planet." And religion has a clear and significant role to play in this transformation.

Religious pluralism, Eboo Patel once said, can "go up in the flames of a suicide bombing. But it also dies in the face of a thousand silent betrayals."[180] Many of us believe that there is an inextricable link between religious faith and social values, between theology and sociology, between the spiritual and the political. But we must have the courage to uphold these values in our lives. If we do not do so we fail society, and we fail God.[181]

Perhaps we need to begin by recognizing that spirituality, or even more importantly religion, is not something that we just 'do' on Sunday, or Saturday, or the Sabbath. I say "more importantly religion" because those of you who are spiritual without seeing the need for religion may feel that you are already practicing your own particular 'brand' of spirituality throughout your lives? But I do not mean just being a spiritual individual, perhaps focusing on personal spiritual growth for personal gain. I mean using an infusion of spirit as a transformative element in everything we do as we go about our daily lives. And the well-established networks and doctrines of the world's religions help us do this.

This is an idea I developed in some more detail in my first book *Healing This Wounded Earth*, while also weaving the vulnerability and compassion of the Wounded Healer into the equation, in the context of politics, economics, business, creativity, leisure, the natural world, community, healthcare and faith.

James Hunter is clearly thinking along similar lines, writing from a Christian perspective in *To Change the World*, when he calls for a "Faithful Presence" specifically among Christians.

Starting with worship, Hunter calls Christians to engage in and with the world around them, among those of any faith or none, and within their own particular spheres of influence to bring their faith of love to the workplace, the arts, architecture, urban planning, news media, academia, and so on. Is this the answer for those 'spiritual but not religious' who left the church to practice a brand of Christianity closer to the teachings of Jesus Christ; for those who feel disenchanted that the church is not taking Jesus Christ out into the world? I think so.

Faithful Presence is a covenantal commitment, Hunter explains, oriented towards a flourishing of the world around us and rooted in the Judeo-Christian idea of justice.

We offer at a minimum, he writes, the gifts of faith, hope and love in the broadest sense, speaking to a basic human need in the whole human community. Through this he calls for an assault on the worldliness of the present age, a bursting out of new creation from within it. We are all followers and leaders in this. Everyone in some large or small way as a Christian is obliged to carry that burden. And it will require creative thinking, imagination and hard work at local parish level, within consortia of congregations, and in denominational bodies. The Church has obligations, he writes, and has the resources to offer this alternative to popular culture.[182] This may seem like what Hunter describes as a quietly radical alternative. But for our Muslim brethren their Islamic faith is very much a part of their living culture, as they demonstrate in their cycle of daily prayer that God should be a part of day-to-day life.

A new religion?

After long study and experience, I have come to the conclusion that (1) all religions are true; (2) all religions have some error in them; (3) all religions are almost as dear to me as my own Hinduism, in as much as all human beings should be as dear to one as one's own close relatives. My own veneration for other faiths is the same as that for my own faith; therefore no thought of conversion is possible.
M.K. Gandhi[183]

If it ain't broke, don't fix it, as the saying goes. Is religion broke? Far from it, although some of the channels need a bit of retuning! Let's tweak the controls of what we have, not set out to throw it all away.

Some call for a universal religion, a kind of 'one size fits all' idea, believing that this would put an end to strife and disagreement! How could this possibly work? Is it possible to have a universal religion?

Apparently the Renaissance Cardinal Nicholas of Cusa suggested a federation of existing faiths, with the idea that their mutual tolerance and improved acquaintanceship may pave the way for a new common world-religion in the future. This would not work, simply because, as Bouquet observed, "each religion is suitable to the people among whom it has developed, but is an exotic elsewhere."[184]

There is in fact a relatively new global religion, the Unitarian Universalist Association of Congregations, a liberal religion rooted in Judaism and Christianity but with no creed of its own. It is really an umbrella organization for those of any faith or belief. In each member congregation, everyone is free to search for his or her own personal truth on the issues that preoccupy all religions, such as the nature and meaning of life, an afterlife and creation. Members can come from any religious or cultural background. Values they promote include the inherent worth and dignity of every person; justice, equity and compassion in human relations; acceptance of one another and encouragement to spiritual growth; a free and responsible search for truth and meaning; with the goal of a world community where all live in peace, liberty and justice, with respect for the interdependent web of all existence of which we are a part.[185]

This idea comes close to Godism, the Reverend Moon's term for a universal religious perspective, embracing the truths of all religions, a perspective which he believes will become the basis for a God-centered, pluralistic society, nation, and world.

But why do we need yet another organization for this?

If we pursue the idea of some kind of universal religion, no one in the view of Pope Benedict XVI offered "a more impressive, warmer or even persuasive picture of a religion of the future" than philosopher and statesman Sarvepalli Radhakrishnan, President of India from 1962 to 1967. His works "ever and again lead up to a vista of the coming religion of the spirit, which will be able to unite fundamental unity with the most varied differentiation," and they come with all the weight of human and religious authority behind them; not only offering a palpable future for religion, but also making the Christian theologian look like "a dogmatic stick in the mud..."[186]

Now that, I think, is what the world needs!

There are very many different ideas and philosophies around life, our spirituality, our religions and our faiths. I've already explored some of these in previous pages. I believe that at the end of the day they are all not so very different from each other. They are all moving towards one common purpose and theme, an overarching spirituality, a pulsating energized mass of humanity all interconnected through a spiritual plane, which is outside the restrictions of time or space.

If this is so, the care of our souls has to be the supreme objective, the priority in our lives. And so we come back to religions, because this of course is their first role above all else. We in turn care for the Earth simply because we love and respect all Creation.[187] Sadly there are some Christians who believe that their personal salvation in the next world matters above all else and there is therefore no need to worry about how they ravage the earth in this life. That cannot be right. Jesus taught compassion for all and that has to include Creation in all its wonderful diversity. So do we save the world or save our souls?

We need to do both.

At the moment I think we are in great danger of doing neither.

Chapter 7

Education for Everyone

Few things are likely to be more important for the 21st century than wise faith among the world's religious communities. That calls for fuller understanding, better education, and a commitment to the flourishing of our whole planet.
Professor David F. Ford, Director of the Cambridge Inter-Faith Programme

I opened this book with the story of Sebaki Tandi, the little seven-month-old orphan girl whose life was turned around when a Christian relief charity stepped in to pay for her education.[188]

I believe education is the key to our future and we don't seem to be doing it very well at the moment. Reliable data is hard to find, but a massive proportion of the world's children, by any standards, receive little or no education at all. The problem is worse among girls, and represents a massive global injustice. Two-thirds of the world's illiterates are female and women tend to bear the responsibility for meeting their families' basic needs. Studies show that when women are supported and empowered, society as a whole benefits; families are healthier, more children go to school, and family income increases.[189] Even among the so-called developed nations, the available education sometimes falls short of an acceptable standard particularly in poor areas.

Basic education must reach the world's women and children. This is urgent. The ability to read and write should be an entitlement for all people.

But I also believe that spiritual literacy is essential for the future; that all young people need to be educated in the ways of spirit and respect and love, because this will be the world's healing force.

Education too often now concentrates only on league tables and exam results; there is too much emphasis on going on to higher education, to being able to command good jobs and high salaries, to rise to the 'top.' And in many schools there is little time or space for spiritual nurture, for soul healing, beyond relativistic religious studies. We have lost the balance between the objective and the subjective, between the exoteric and the esoteric, between thinking and feeling. That's a shame because spirituality comes naturally to the very young. I observe this first hand in my work in an Anglican church with its own Church School. Young children have what has been described as a "pure love, a simplicity of openness and an innate spirituality."[190] And there is plenty of scientific evidence that supports this. Humans appear to be born with an inbuilt spiritual awareness, and this will normally be expressed via the religious culture in which they are nurtured.[191] The big question for spiritual educators is how they retain that innate spirituality in children. The great tragedy is that it seems to be very often left at the school gates when children enter secondary school.

The Dalai Lama stresses that education "constitutes one of our most powerful weapons in our quest to bring about a better, more peaceful, world."[192] He emphasizes the need to open children's eyes to the needs and rights of others, so that their actions have a universal dimension, and they develop their "natural feelings of empathy so that they come to have a sense of responsibility towards others." He reminds us that traditionally it has been assumed that ethical and human values would be taught through a child's religious upbringing rather than in mainstream state education. With the declining influence of religion and faith in family life this vital part of a child's education has become neglected. The Dalai Lama proffers three guidelines for the education of our children. First, he says, we need to awaken their consciousness to basic human values by showing them how these are relevant to their future survival, rather than presenting them as solely an ethical or faith issue. Then we must teach them how to discuss and debate, to understand the value of dialogue rather than violence for resolving conflict. Finally there is the urgent need to teach children that differences of race, faith, culture, while important to preserve, are nevertheless secondary to the equal rights of us all from whatever background to be happy.

The former Assistant Secretary General of the United Nations and later Chancellor of Costa Rica's Peace University, Robert Muller, wrote in the 1980s of the need for a global education that "must transcend material, scientific and intellectual achievements and reach deliberately into the moral and spiritual spheres." After extending the power of our hands with incredible machines, our eyes with telescopes and microscopes, our ears with cell phones, radio and sonar, our brains with computers and automation, he wrote, we must now also extend our hearts, our feelings, our love, and our soul "to the entire human family, to the planet, to the stars, to the universe, to eternity and to God."[193]

Why does so much wisdom get lost within the mists of time?

The Global Justice Movement describes the purpose of education as to "teach people how to become life-long learners and virtuous human beings, with the capacity to adapt to change, to become masters of technology and builders of civilization through their 'leisure work', and to pursue the highest spiritual values."[194]

Many other respected thinkers are calling for a spiritual revolution in our schools, a move towards an education that enhances spiritual literacy.[195]

Let's now do something about it.

I've already mentioned that the world's religions have an enormous influence in education. And where they are involved, and use that mandate for proper spiritual nurture and growth, rather than for any subversive activity, then all to the well and good. And of course it is the perceived indoctrination and exclusivity, for good or ill, of 'religious' schools that the atheists rail against.

So let's take a little space to look at some of the spiritual and holistic education that is taking place in the world right now.

I said before that our local church school is over subscribed. I would hazard an informed guess that parents send children there for the spiritual values it teaches. I see nothing wrong with that.

Hindus place great emphasis on the importance of a holistic education for their children, so that their values are rooted in spirituality. Recognizing the destruction caused by ignorance, emphasis is placed on Hindu education from an early age, not only in the school but also in the family unit and in the community. Traditional Hindu education covers all aspects of life, including economic, political, cultural, and above all the religious. For a Hindu "the body and mind are in the service of the heart. In the same way politics and economics are rooted in and guided by religion and culture, and ultimately by spiritual experience."[196]

Rudolf Steiner was probably one of the first to see the danger of education being driven more by the economic needs of society than the interests of the child. He believed strongly in an education to develop the child's intellectual, creative and moral well-being, in an atmosphere of cooperation and love rather than competition. To some his ideas and methods are controversial. But the number of Waldorf and Rudolf Steiner schools worldwide is testament to the success of his formula. For example at the time of writing there are some 130 in the US, 227 in Germany, 92 in the Netherlands, 41 in Sweden and more than 30 in the United Kingdom. And the organization is growing fast.[197] I have visited such a school and was enormously impressed by the thoroughly pleasant, well grounded and well educated young citizens there, seemingly untarnished by many of the distractions to be observed outside the school gates of some if not most of our secular secondary schools. We need well-rounded, happy, respectful, empathic and spiritual citizens.

Environmental activist Alastair McIntosh has a vision for a spiritually rich and holistic education. He imagines a life-long curriculum of organic food and biodiversity, energy alternatives and respect for all, healing skills incorporating not only the most advanced scientific advances but also the spiritual healing principles, of poetry and story. And there would be the study of conflict resolution and how to eliminate the causes of war. McIntosh's education vision is about "building of *community* as right relationship between soil, soul and society, powered by the passion of the heart, steered by the reason of the head, and then applied by the skilled technique of the hand."[198]

James D'Angelo calls for us to include the spiritual life as a priority in education for future generations, in an education "that reveals the illusion of the material world and the reality of our eternal nature."[199] This would include meditation, aided by yoga and tai chi, for example, along with prayer, the idea of holding someone in a mental plane, the "contemplation of spiritual knowledge," the participation in artistic activity and learning to be of service to others.

So many respected people and organizations are promoting the need for a more holistic and spiritual education for our children and youth. This need becomes ever more urgent: we must give them all the encouragement and support possible. At our own local level this is a wonderful opportunity for school governors, teachers and parents to influence the spiritual education of our children for the future of our world.

We can all benefit from a holistic education. The religions nurture the spiritual growth of their followers, the spiritual but not religious are similarly seeking spiritual growth in some shape or form, for a variety of purposes. Education can be a holistic journey of spiritual discovery and growth, a development of body, mind and spirit for us all, as we all learn how to become fully human. And religion can and should be there to help us along that journey.

I am hopeful that the organized religions are here to stay. That is not to say that we cannot be critical of some of their activities, of some of their doctrines and dogma. But we can support the good in them. They have a very valuable role to play in education in nurturing that true spirituality that is the hope for our world.

Chapter 8

Conclusion

So let our differences not cause hatred and strife between us. Let us vie with each other only in righteousness and good works. Let us respect each other, be fair, just and kind to [one] another and live in sincere peace, harmony and mutual goodwill.

From *A Common Word Between Us and You*, an open letter to all leaders of the Christian churches and denominations worldwide, signed by 138 leading Muslim scholars and intellectuals, October 2007.

The challenges that the world currently faces are many.

And religions have a huge role to play. They are social and spiritual capital writ large.

I have written about the need for the churches and other places of worship to change, of the need for educational reform, for media cooperation, for dialogue and humility.

And while to an extent we can blame scientific advances for the lost credibility that religions face in the Western world, science ironically may be providing some of the tools for religious tolerance at the level of our mind and soul.

The wonderful messages of love and affirmation, forgiveness and healing of a gentle Jesus were feminine goddess qualities brought into the harsh patriarchal world of that time. It has been suggested that the "brute forces of patriarchal mentality... struck back and suppressed and intimidated the forces of love."[200] Moreover, the Church has failed to protest sufficiently throughout its existence against what Skolimowski (2010) calls the perversion of Christ's teachings. Why? Because, he writes, the status quo has always been male dominated, patriarchal, and that is why "the great religion of love [is] limping." And the Christian churches will not strengthen and renew themselves, he writes, until they cease to ally themselves with the dominant male status quo, they cease to worship Mammon, and they truly recognize the female side of Jesus and pursue love (and to that I would add spirituality) beyond all else in their teaching and actions. Interesting thoughts indeed, when we consider that we are in a period of global financial turmoil, capitalism protest demonstrations have taken place on Wall Street and far beyond, female priests play an increasingly important role in many churches and indeed the first female primate in the Anglican Communion, the presiding bishop of the Episcopal Church, is a woman, and it seems that at last we may see female bishops in the Church of England before too long.[201]

There are thousands of organizations large and small that work tirelessly across the world to keep the principles of religious pluralism alive. In the USA alone more than 1000 such organizations are promoting inter-faith cooperation. They need our support.

But this is all at the exoteric level. Alongside a greater under-standing of consciousness than even a few years ago, many[202] are calling for a more integral spirituality, which can generate the energy needed to touch people at a deep esoteric level, believing that anger and pain can stir enthusiasm for real healing action where governance is failing. Others emphasize the need for our race to mature, to move from egocentric immaturity, focused on our own selves, through a mind-focused ethnocentric adoles-cence, to world centric and Cosmic centric maturity, or full spiritual integration. Ken Wilber[203] with his spiritual mapping techniques explains why he thinks that religion "is the only insti-tution in all of humanity's endeavors" that can fulfill this. Pope Benedict XVI writes that God has to reappear in a convincing fashion to the world[204] and urges us to bring reason and religion together again for the sake of man and for the sake of the world.

We need to kindle spiritualities, heighten our awareness and sensibilities, find a sense of global responsibility and a new kind of spiritual literacy.[205] And in this the religions have a most vital role to play.

So we see revised worldviews and new ideas emerging to address the problems that concern so many of us.

What else do we need to do?

We need to foster wisdom above knowledge

In Plato's *Phaedrus*, the "father of letters" Thoth comes to tell the Egyptian King Thutmose about his new invention, the art of writing. This will help the Egyptians remember things, and will make them wise, he said. But Thutmose was not impressed. "This will create forgetfulness in the learners' souls," he said, "because they will not use their memories; they will trust to the external written characters and not remember of themselves. The specific which you have discovered is an aid not to memory, but to reminiscence, and you give your disciples not truth, but only the semblance of truth; they will be hearers of many things and will have learned nothing."[206]

We have huge amounts of knowledge or information freely available to us but we really do not know what to do with much of it and it is not nourishing the spiritual within us. We need wisdom. And knowledge is not wisdom. Only critical consideration and deep thinking over time bring wisdom. And as I have said before, wisdom is so often lost and forgotten rather than savored and utilized for the common good of all humanity.

The Internet can be a wonderful tool but a dangerous one. Those not taught in the skills of discriminatory research or the ability to think can surf the web, absorb whatever they find and regurgitate quantities of it without a further thought for its accuracy or provenance. What is worse, many suddenly seem to claim huge expertise on something about which they really know very little. And we become surrounded with bigotry and aggression, intolerance and ridicule, fuelled by the web's easy accessibility and relative anonymity: and it is really not good for us.[207]

> Intellect is arrogant and immodest. When critical it rends and ravishes.Wisdom is meek and chaste. When understanding, it heals and unifies. The open-minded enquiry is a wise enquiry, reverent and grateful. One of its faithful servants is doubt, the humble but searching doubt of truth-seeking. It challenges all authority, but not with the insolent self-assertiveness of the ignorant.[208]

It would be good for us all if we heed such wise, indeed profound, words.

We all of us need humility. We need less cynicism, although a little is healthy and essential! We need to understand that we simply do not know what we do not know. We have tried too hard to understand things we shall never understand, and to know things we shall never know.

Martin Luther King once said that nothing in the entire world is more dangerous than sincere ignorance and conscientious stupidity. We need neither.

We need wisdom.

And we need to use crisis as opportunity

There are many who believe that we actually need a serious crisis before we are really motivated sufficiently to pull together for a common cause. Those old enough will recall the cooperation within communities during World War II. Even individually, some of us find that revision for that looming exam becomes more intense and focused only as the date draws closer, when it is almost too late for any meaningful and lasting learning.

The socio-economic, ecological and spiritual challenges of the present day are an opportunity for us all to do something, to consider how a new integration of science, philosophy and ancient spiritual wisdom may be brought about: to promote a new worldview of harmony between all sentient beings, an enhancement of wisdom and a balance between matter and spirit, head and heart. And in doing so it is incumbent on us all that we should not devalue the vital role religions can play, now and in the future.[209]

We need to understand that each individual is a unique spiritual mystery, and we must be prepared not only to make dialogue with others outside our own limited circle but also to see each other as divine and be prepared to then change ourselves at some deep level. We are now profoundly connected as humans across the world, and action is urgent. But we are guilty of a kind of group egotism, often loving only our own kind. Augustine saw that the State which looked after only its own interests rather than pursuing a justice for all was no more than an organized band of robbers. Sometimes I think that we are like that band of robbers. We need to look not only to universal justice now, but we need to look to the future with new eyes.

A rule of the ascetic Jains is for 'Careful Actions, Careful Thoughts.' Here is a good guide for living for us all. Before taking any action we need to ask ourselves what effect that action will have on us, on others, on society, on the planet and on a generation or more from now. This type of thinking is instinctive in many indigenous cultures. It underpins the Seventh Generation Principle, from the political culture of the Iroquois people, and now adopted by Native American elders and activists. "What about the seventh generation? Where are you taking them? What will they have?"

So I hope in this short book I have managed to show why religion is still important and why its many organizations and efforts for humanity need everyone's support. To the atheists, I would say that you do not have to believe in God; that is your choice. But please leave the religions alone. Please respect where we are coming from and don't feel you have to join a crusade of abuse, a quest for the abolition of religion. Because such a crusade could prove as deadly and costly to mankind as the original Crusades you so vehemently criticize.

Whether we like it or not, religion is here to stay, certainly for the duration of the time frame that we probably have left to steer our own evolution in a better direction than its present trajectory. And religions will be an essential part of that evolution.

At the end of the day our religions do underpin values for very many people, and our values distinguish the human from the subhuman. We must live ecologically and we need to live as mature humans. So many have traveled different pathways to come to the same conclusion. Mehta commented that when we consider the environment, the institutions and ourselves, we have least power over nature, most power over ourselves.[210] Therefore it is we who need to change. As Gandhi so famously said in probably one of the most oft quoted wisdoms of our time, "You must be the change you want to see in the world." And in changing ourselves we ignore the wisdoms of the ancient religions at our peril.

Everything now depends on man… Immense power of destruction is given into his hands, and the question is whether he can resist the will to use it, and can temper his will with the spirit of love and wisdom. He will hardly be able to do so on his own resources. He needs the help of an 'advocate' in heaven.[211]

Carl G. Jung

Notes

1   Story reproduced with permission by email January 11, 2012 from *Transmission* Spring 2012, the newspaper of USPG: Anglicans in World Mission, p. 4.

2   Palmer with Finlay (2003) p. 3.

3   The Qur'an 007.031.

4   And this is not confined to Christianity; Islam has the same problem.

5   Stoneham (2011).

6   Putnam and Campbell (2010) Ch. 1 at note 5.

7   http://www.whychurch.org.uk/trends.php citing an original 2007 Tearfund report also at http://news.bbc .co.uk/2/shared/bsp/hi/pdfs/03_04_07_tearfundchurch.pdf sourced February 27, 2012.

8   For further discussion on this see Ian Christie article on the global reality of faith, "A World of Faith," in "Moving Mountains: How Can Faith Shape Our Future?" editor Anna Simpson, *Green Futures*, 2011.

9   Sam Harris (2005) Epilogue p. 223 for example seems to believe that religion could be abolished in a single generation if all parents simply gave honest answers to their children's questions and did not brainwash them with religious education – but he does concede that this is probably a hopeless dream, acknowledging the sheer scale of global religious belief!

10 Readers can find detailed academic treatment of spirituality in the *Journal for the Study of Spirituality*, volume 1.1 launched 2011.

11 For further reading on this I recommend Spencer and Alexander (2009).

12 Teilhard de Chardin (1978) p. 191.

13 Story taken from website of Episcopal Relief and

Development, Healing a Hurting World http://www.erd.org/with email permission March 21, 2012.

14   green change website http://www.greenchange.org/article.php?id=5302 sourced October 31, 2011.

15   Spirit in Nature website http://www.spiritinnature.com/index.shtml sourced February 26, 2012.

16   The Forum on Religion and Ecology at Yale http://fore.research.yale.edu/ sourced February 25, 2012.

17   Alliance of Religions and Conservation (ARC) http://www.arcworld.org/news.asp?pageID=484 "Ten faith traditions have nominated pilgrim cities or sacred sites to become founding members of the Green Pilgrimage Network, ranging as far afield as Louguan in the People's Republic of China for Daoists to St Albans in the UK for Anglicans and Amritsar for the Sikhs. The city authorities of Jerusalem, a major pilgrimage destination for three faiths, Judaism, Christianity and Islam, will join the network to green the city for all pilgrims... Other founder members of The Green Pilgrimage Network include... the Coptic Orthodox Church, which will green its St Bishoy Monastery at Wadi El Natroun in Egypt, visited by some 100,000 mainly Coptic Orthodox pilgrims every summer; Jinja Honcho, the Association of Shinto shrines in Japan, responsible for around 80,000 shrines, including many in forests that are the dwelling places of kami deities." Sourced February 27, 2012.

18   Stoneham (2011).

19   ARC http://www.arcworld.org/news.asp?pageID=485 sourced 26 February, 2012. "Chinese government consults the Daoists on social problems for the first time in 900 years."

20   A good place to start is with the Forum on Religion and Ecology at Yale http://fore.research.yale.edu/. See also http://eenonline.org/, http://eqat.wordpress.com/, http://www.arrcc.org.au/ and http://www.ecen.org/ all sourced February 26, 2012.

21 Penney Poyzer,TV broadcaster and writer, and Chris Goodall, *Independent on Sunday* and author of *How to Live a Low-Carbon Life*, in "The Fifty Things That Will Save the Planet," An Environment Agency Survey 2007, http://publications.environment-agency.gov.uk/PDF/GEHO0907BNFQ-E-E.pdf sourced February 16, 2012.22

22 To this end many cross cultural, interfaith conferences convene to move environmental initiatives forward. See for example Sustainability in Crisis, September 2010, organized jointly by the Kirby Laing Institute for Christian Ethics (KLICE), and the Faraday Institute for Science and Religion, both of which have close links with the Christian community; but speakers came from not only Christian but also Islamic, Buddhist, and secular backgrounds. Scientists and students, many at the cutting edge of current research into climate change issues, alongside ordained Christian ministers, Muslims, representatives of charities, NGOs, and more, over 100 delegates, gathered together to help achieve the two goals of the conference; firstly "to identify key sustainable and realizable policy changes for the next decade, at three levels: consumption, production, governance," and secondly "to consider how to enlist the critical support of religious communities behind these changes." The project is ongoing at http://sustainabilityincrisis.word press.com/ April 27, 2012.

23 These being morality, religious observance, posture, control of Life Energy (or breath-control), withdrawal of senses from worldly objects (detachment), collectedness of mind, meditation, mental union of meditated with meditator from Mehta (1987) p. 256. Morality is further defined in the Sandilya Upanishad 1.13 as harmlessness, truth, non-covetousness, continence, kindliness, equanimity, patient endurance, steadiness of mind in gain and loss, abstemiousness (especially with food and drink) and clean-

liness of body and mind.

24   Mehta (1987) pp. 258, 259.

25   Several translations are available on the Internet see for example http://www.accesstoinsight.org/tipitaka/mn/mn. 021x.budd.html or http://wisdomquarterly.blogspot.com/20 09/10/saw-and-other-parables.html sourced February 26, 2012.

26   His Holiness the 14th Dalai Lama (2000) p. 19. Cited in Armstrong (2011) p. 20.

27   His Holiness the 14th Dalai Lama (2000) p. 11.

28   Martin Luther King, Nobel Peace Prize Lecture December 11, 1964.

29   Grayling (2004) pp. 80–81.

30   Wilson, editor (1991) p. 27.

31   http://www.unification.net/ws/ sourced February 26, 2012. The fact that this was commissioned by the controversial and colorful Reverend Sun Myung Moon (in 1985) should not be allowed to detract from the value of this useful volume.

32   http://www.unification.net/ws/wsessay.htm sourced February 26, 2012.

33   http://www.americanrhetoric.com/speeches/mlkatimeto-breaksilence.htm sourced February 26, 2012.

34   Although I should perhaps point out here that both the Buddha and Meister Eckhart praise detachment over love.

35   Martin Buber as quoted in Diamond (2002) p. 78.

36   Exodus 20:1–17 and Deuteronomy 5:4–2.

37   Cited in Wilson, editor (1991).

38   Palmer with Finlay (2003). Material in this book on the creeds of the different world faiths relating to their care of creation are from the statements compiled specifically by those faiths for the Alliance of Religions and Conservation (ARC) and included in this book by Palmer and Finlay. The statements are freely quoted with the explicit permission of

all parties involved in their production. As the authors point out, no one owns the wisdom of the faiths any more than we can own creation itself. I do acknowledge with thanks the use of all such material. The information is available in full on the ARC website and generally on the individual faith websites, as well as in the book *Faith in Conservation*. I also acknowledge the authors of each faith statement as appropriate in these endnotes.

39 I explored this in very much more detail in Stoneham (2011), in the context of environmental issues and climate change.

40 http://www.ifees.org.uk/ sourced October 31, 2011.

41 From Simpson, editor (2011) Fazlun Khalid, Founder and Director of IFEES, "Creation Works as a Whole," p. 9.

42 From the Sikh faith statement compiled by Sri Akhal Takhat Sahib under the guidance of Sri Singh Sahib Manjit Singh, the Jathedar of Anandapur, for Palmer with Finlay (2003) pp. 132, 134.

43 From the Hindu faith statement written for Palmer with Finlay (2003) pp. 91, 93 which consists of three distinct sections reflecting the major strands within Vedic (Hindu) thought – these quotations are from the statement based on the comments by: Swami Vibudhesha Teertha, Acharya of Madhvacarya Vaishnavas, Udupi, Central Advisory Committee Member of the Visva Hindu Parishad. Also at http://www.arcworld.org/faiths.asp?pageID=77 sourced February 26, 2012.

44 The Buddhist faith statement for the ARC was prepared by Kevin Fossey, Buddhist educator and representative of Engaged Buddhism in Europe; Somdech Preah Maha Ghosananda, Patriarch of Cambodian Buddhism; His Excellency Sri Kushok Bakula, 20th Reincarnation of the Buddha's Disciple Bakula, head of Ladakhi Buddhism, and initial rebuilder of Mongolian Buddhism; and Venerable

Nhem Kim Teng, Patriarch of Vietnamese Buddhism: from Palmer and Finlay (2003) pp. 77, 78. Also at http://www. arcworld.org/faiths.asp?pageID=66 sourced February 26, 2012.

45 Very much the theme of Stoneham (2011).

46 Palmer with Finlay (2003). The statement on Christianity was compiled and endorsed by the Ecumenical Patriarchate of Constantinople, the World Council of Churches, and the Vatican Franciscan Center of Environmental Studies. Quotations from pp. 83–85.

47 RSV Hebrews 13:2.

48 For more on Islamic hospitality see *Hospitality: A Worldwide Islamic Tradition* 2005 http://www.spcm.org/monthdetails/ 2005/md-May-2005.html sourced February 26, 2012.

49 See for example SikhNet, Sharing the Sikh Experience, http://www.sikhnet.com/news/united-sikh-association-serves-langar-nyu-students sourced February 26, 2012 and at http://hinduism.iskcon.com/lifestyle/810.htm

50 Mahabharata 12.374 cited at http://hinduism.iskcon.com /lifestyle/810.htm sourced February 26, 2012.

51 Bouquet (1953) p. 25.

52 Skolimowski (2010) pp. 103, 104.

53 Holy Bible, Joshua chapters 13 to 21.

54 Ibid Leviticus 25.

55 Ibid Leviticus 25:10.

56 Ibid Jeremiah 31:17.

57 Stoneham (2011).

58 Aristotle (1998) 1.9 1258a 35 p. 30.

59 Rankin (2010).

60 Skolimowski, 2010) p. 109. These paths have various names, for example, Grace in the Christian culture, *Satori* (Zen Buddhism), *Samadhi* (Hinduism), and *Bodhisattva* (Mahayana Buddhism).

61 Cited in Ratzinger (2005) p. 176, the oration of 384 by the

senator Symacchus quoted from Gnilka, Chresis also pp. 19–26 for detailed analysis of text.

62   From the statement compiled under the guidance of Sri Singh Sahib Manjit Singh, the Jathedar of Anandapur, who is one of the five spiritual and temporal heads of Sikhism; and Sri Akhal Takhat Sahib, his deputy. From Palmer and Finlay (2003) p. 141 and at http://www.arcworld.org/faiths.asp?pageID=73 sourced February 26, 2012.

63   http://www.gandhi-manibhavan.org/gandhiphilosophy/philosophy_god_gospeloffaith.htm Gandhi's *Views On God – The Gospel of Faith*. Sourced February 26, 2012.

64   Mehta (1987) pp. 261, 256, 27.

65   I owe much of the detail and ideas in this section on Darwinism to the excellent essay by Spencer and Alexander (2009).

66   Spencer and Alexander (2009) p. 33.

67   Writer of recommended textbooks who took her own life in Amsterdam in May 2006 age 58.

68   Spencer and Alexander (2009).

69   Dr. Edgar Mitchell, Apollo 14 astronaut, http://www.space-quotations.com/earth.html sourced February 26 2012 cites *The Way of the Explorer: An Apollo Astronaut's Journey Through the Material and Mystical Worlds*, New Page Books; Revised edition (February 15, 2008).

70   His Holiness the 14th Dalai Lama (2000) p. 11.

71   The first monotheistic religion, which influenced the three Abrahamic faiths and whose doctrine is "good thoughts, good words, good deeds."

72   Mehta (1987) pp. 271, 278.

73   For example see Spencer and Alexander (2009) and Polkinghorne (1986).

74   Sheldrake (2012).

75   Institute of Noetic Sciences http://www.noetic.org/.

76   http://www.noetic.org/research/project/spiritual-engag

ement-project/ sourced February 26, 2012.

77 http://www.bbc.co.uk/news/science-environment-15017484 sourced October 13, 2011.

78 Ludwig Wittgenstein from his Tractatus Logico-Philosophicus, 1992.

79 Clarke (2010) p. 110.

80 Gilbert (2010) pp. 505–509.

81 Tomlinson (2008).

82 Richard Dawkins and Steven Pinker, 1999, public debate on 10th February 1999 at Westminster Central Hall, London, "Is Science Killing the Soul?", reported in *Edge* 53, 8 April 1999, at http://www.edge.org/documents/archive/edge53.html sourced February 26, 2012.

83 Dawkins (2006).

84 Medawar (1979).

85 See for example: Flew (2007), Lennox (2007), Williams (2009), McGrath (2005), McGrath and McGrath (2007).

86 For further reading I would recommend Sacks (2011).

87 Polkinghorne (1986) chapter 3, "The Nature of Theology."

88 A theme incidentally also explored in some detail by Mehta (1987) p. 269 ff.

89 Ratzinger (2005) p. 17.

90 Niebuhr (2009).

91 Sourced from Niebuhr (2009) p. xxviii/xxix.

92 http://www.archbishopofcanterbury.org/ sourced February 26, 2012.

93 Niebuhr (2009) p. xvi.

94 Rankin (2010).

95 Hsiang, Meng and Cane, in *Nature* August 2011 cited at http://motherjones.com/blue-marble/2011/08/climate-change-war-el-nino and pdf at https://motherjones.com/files/nature10311.pdf "Civil conflicts are associated with the global climate" sourced February 26, 2012.

96 Niebuhr (2009) p. xviii.

97   Although there is a story in *The Times* November 25, 2011 from Los Angeles of a renegade Amish splinter sect in Ohio numbering about 120 persons who have made violent attacks against other Amish communities following criticism of the sect by Amish bishops.

98   Armstrong (2011) p. 7.

99   Volf, bin Muhammad and Yarrington, editors (2010) p. 6.

100   Esposito and Mogahed (2008), a seminal book, the results of probably the largest international religious survey ever.

101   See for example http://www.tektonics.org/scim/science mony.htm sourced February 28, 2012.

102   http://pewresearch.org/databank/dailynumber/?Numb erID=509 sourced February 28, 2012.

103   http://datinggod.org/2010/10/05/dear-sam-harris-please-act ually-study-religion/ sourced February 28, 2012.

104   See for example http://www.rationalskepticism.org/chris tianity/how-many-christians-are-young-earth-creationists-t6197.html February 28, 2012.

105   Darrell Williams: "Religious Wars and the Fallacies of Fundamentalism" September 2007 in *American Chronicle* http://www.americanchronicle.com/articles/view/38605 sourced April 27, 2012.

106   Grayling (2004) pp. 5–6.

107   Stoneham (2011) where in Chapter 9 I explored in some detail the responsibility of creativity, including the media.

108   See http://www.thenews.com.pk/TodaysPrintDetail.aspx?I D=68512&Cat=3 sourced February 28, 2012.

109   http://www.pensitoreview.com/2008/02/27/poll-majority-muslims-worldwide-condemn-9-11/ sourced February 28, 2012.

110   Niebuhr (2009) p. 9.

111   Although in Miroslav Volf, *A Common Word* 2010, at p. 5 HRH Prince Ghazi Bin Muhammad of Jordan writes that from a cursory review of Amazon.com Americans "are

buying more books about Islam written by vitriolic former Muslims now touted as experts and sponsored by Christian fundamentalist groups than written by serious Muslims or non-Muslim scholars." This is clearly not a helpful sign.

112 Grayling (2004) p. 80 and Chapter 4 generally.

113 Thomas Paine in *The Rights of Man* on religious toleration: cited in Hardy (2011).

114 Charles Bonney, 1893 Protestant involved in founding the World Parliament of Religions, now the Parliament of the World's Religions.

115 Warning over 100 years ago by the great African-American scholar W.E.B. Du Bois see Du Bois (2011).

116 Eboo Patel (2007) and also by Eboo Patel "Building the Beloved Community; Values of Religious Pluralism" in *Frank, the magazine of the Clinton School of Public Service* (2007) p. 58, http://www.clintonschool.uasys.edu/frank-magazine/ sourced April 27, 2012.

117 Interfaith Youth Core www.ifyc.org sourced February 28, 2012.

118 Interfaith Youth Core International Work Summary at http://www.ifyc.org/sites/default/files/u4/Int%27l%20Projec ts%20Resume%5B1%5D.pdf sourced February 28, 2012.

119 http://www.nobelprize.org/nobel_prizes/peace/laureate s/1964/king-lecture.html sourced February 28, 2012.

120 http://www.gestalt.ie/further-reading/page-4.asp sourced February 28, 2012. This was the famous idea developed by the existentialist philosopher Martin Buber (1937) on the interrelationship that may form between two people. Buber said there are three types of dialogue: the genuine, the technical and the monologue disguised as dialogue, and it is the genuine dialogue that has the maximum power to heal, and is clearly of most relevance to fostering religious respect and understanding.

121 Volf, bin Muhammad and Yarrington, editors (2010) p. 26.

122 Nurani.org sourced February 28, 2012.

123 Ibid.

124 Nurani is supported by the Coexist Foundation which "recognises and celebrates the many connections between the Abrahamic faiths, whilst acknowledging their differences and distinctiveness." http://www.coexistfounda tion.net/ sourced February 28, 2012. The foundation is built on the premise that we learn more about ourselves and our own traditions by looking respectfully at others and so build good relations between the two.

125 Cited by Niebuhr (2009) p. 105, as acts for creating spiritual intimacy between different faiths outside an evangelical context.

126 Niebuhr (2009) p. xxvii.

127 In this excellent book, by Gustav Niebuhr 2009, he provides plenty of illustrative stories of cross religion initiatives, of religions coming together to serve others, of cooperating on social projects, sharing places of worship, assisting with rebuilding programs of mosques, churches, synagogues, etc, as well as promoting dialogue. Although primarily about religion in America, where it is a source of public identity for many, the interest in this book should not be so confined. The issues are, after all, global.

128 See also for example Hampton (2010).

129 From www.nurani.org sourced February 28, 2011, an online bilingual forum for facilitating dialogue between Muslim, Jews and Christians.

130 Volf, bin Muhammad and Yarrington, editors (2010) p. 51.

131 Ibid, p. 214 App. 12.

132 A second Muslim-Christian forum was held November 2011 and its statement of mutual agreement "furthering mutual understanding, and advancing the common good of all humanity, especially its yearning for peace, justice and solidarity" is set out at http://www.acommonword.

com/docs/FinalDeclarationEN.pdf and see also the official website of A Common Word at http://www.acommon word.com/index.php?lang=en&page=option1 sourced February 28, 2012.

133 The Cambridge Interfaith Programme http://www.inter-faith.cam.ac.uk/ sourced February 28, 2012.

134 King (2009) pp. 75–76.

135 Documented for example by contributing authors in Lorimer and Robinson, editors (2010).

136 Jung *Answer to Job*, cited in Gilbert (2010) p. 133.

137 *Journal for the Study of Spirituality* volume 1.1, 2011, p. 98 Hunt 2005: 22–26 – citing McBeis' article.

138 For example Drane (2005).

139 For example King (2009) pp. 2–11 and p. 33 et seq.

140 Elkins et al *Journal for the Study of Spirituality* volume 1.1, 2011, p. 58.

141 Pattison (2007) pp. 132–143, "Dumbing Down the Spirit." Cited by John Williams p.100 *JSS*. And furthermore have little to do with the Christian tradition of Spirit and spirituality, which Pattison describes as "altogether more uncom-fortable, astringent, challenging and *world-focussed*" (my italics).

142 *Journal for the Study of Spirituality* volume 1.1, 2011 p. 20.

143 I am grateful to the British Association for the Study of Spirituality and to the various contributors to the first volume of its own academic *Journal for the Study of Spirituality (JSS)*, which was published in 2011. By then the writing of this book was well advanced. Some of the excellent papers were of assistance in pulling together some of my doubts and uncertainties into a more coherent whole. Full recognition has been given in these endnotes as appro-priate.

144 Ursula King, "Can Spirituality Transform our World?" *JSS*, volume 1.1, 2011, p. 19.

145 John Williams, "From Habitus to Critique," in *JSS*, volume 1.1, 2011, p. 99.

146 Astley (2002) p. 39, cited by John Williams in "From Habitus to Critique," in *JSS* p. 99.

147 Pattison (2007) p. 138.

148 Ibid, p. 133, cited p. 100 *JSS*.

149 Ursula King develops this theme in "Can Spirituality Transform our World?" *JSS* (2011) pp. 17 and 22–25.

150 Hick (2004).

151 James D'Angelo essay in Lorimer and Robinson, editors (2010) "A Pathway Towards the One True Religion and Spirituality" p. 209 where he sets out 6 precepts for this.

152 Foster (2010) p. 34–35.

153 http://www.christiansawakening.org/About_CANA.html sourced February 28, 2012 and http://www.wccm.org/home sourced April 27, 2012.

154 For example http://www.st-james-piccadilly.org/WhoWe Are.html sourced February 28, 2012.

155 See research on the Internet as a spiritual network by Heidi Campbell (2005) cited by King in *JSS* 2011 p. 26.

156 http://www.deanradin.com/NewWeb/bio.html and http://thebrowser.com/interviews/larry-dossey-on-premonitions sourced February 28, 2012.

157 Spirituality and Practice http://www.spiritualityandpr actice.com/teachers/teachers.php?id=256 sourced February 28, 2012.

158 Dossey (1989).

159 Definitions of the 3 Eras taken from Larry Dossey article, "The Forces of Healing: Reflections on Energy, Consciousness, and the Beef Stroganoff Principle," revised from the keynote address and welcome originally presented at Exploring the Forces of Healing, the Second Annual *Alternative Therapies* Symposium, April 1997, Orlando, FL.

160 http://noetic.org/research/program/consciousness-healing/

with detailed information and research results on distance healing, sourced February 28, 2012.

161 Dawkins (2006) p. 66.

162 Story related in Dossey (2000) p. 53.

163 See for example Helen Phillips, *New Scientist*, 1 September 2007, pp. 32–36, as cited in Lennox (2011) p. 75.

164 Professor of Psychiatry & Behavioral Sciences and Associate Professor of Medicine, Dr. Koenig is founder and former director of Duke University's Center for the Study of Religion, Spirituality and Health, and is founding Co-Director of the current Center for Spirituality, Theology and Health at Duke University's Medical Center, http://www.spiritualityandhealth.duke.edu/sth/index.html sourced February 28, 2012.

165 Koenig and McConnell (2001).

166 Koenig (2004).

167 Themesa Neckles writes of surrendering to the Holy Spirit in her work, "'… And This Too Shall Pass!' Spiritual Striving and the Academic Life of Three Women." *JSS* (2011) p. 119.

168 Newberg research discussed in some detail in Drane (2005) pp. 73, 74.

169 See also Stoneham (2011).

170 Harvey (2009).

171 For an easy read autobiographical story see Morrison (2011).

172 Indeed that was what inspired me to write my own first book, *Healing This Wounded Earth*. I share that frustration with Karen: about our bad behavior and general lack of responsibility, our lack of knowledge and unthinking actions. So my book complements everything that the Charter stands for, and is about what everyone can do, linking our actions always to compassion and spirit and showing where we can nurture it in our lives. (Although actually it is perhaps more about what we must refrain from doing!) I am pleased that people are buying it. I pray that

they convert ideas into action!

173 An organization dedicated to fostering awareness of the power of love and forgiveness in the world.

174 Charter for Compassion http://charterforcompassion.org /site/ sourced February 28, 2012.

175 Percy Bysshe Shelley, "A Defence of Poetry," http://www. bartleby.com/27/23.html sourced February 28, 2012.

176 Center for Building a Culture of Empathy http:// CultureOfEmpathy.com sourced February 28, 2012 and behind this is http://edwinrutsch.wordpress.com/ and Let's Find 1 Million People Who Want to Build a Culture of Empathy and Compassion, http://Causes.com/Empathy.

177 Lorimer (1990).

178 http://www.resurgence.org/satish-kumar/ sourced February 28, 2012.

179 King (2009) pp. 29, 181.

180 Niebuhr (2009) p. 84.

181 The Rt. Reverend James Jones, Bishop of Liverpool, in the Foreword to Schluter and Ashcroft, editors (2005) p. 11.

182 Hunter (2010).

183 Gandhi (1958) p 60.

184 Bouquet (1953) pp. 295 and 21.

185 Unitarian Universalist site at http://www.uua.org/beliefs /principles/ sourced February 28, 2012.

186 Ratzinger (2005) p. 24 and he recommends the following works of Sarvepalli Radhakrishnan: *The Hindu View of Life* (1926), *An Idealist View of Life* (1929), *Eastern Religions and Western Thought* (1939), Oxford University Press, *Religion and Society* (1947), George Allen and Unwin Ltd, London, *Recovery of Faith* (1956).

187 James D'Angelo, 'A Pathway towards the one true religion and spirituality,' in Lorimer and Robinson, editors (2010) p. 208.

188 Story reproduced with permission January 11, 2012 from

Transmission Spring 2012, the newspaper of USPG: Anglicans in World Mission, p. 4.

189 USPG *Transmission* Autumn 2011 p. 2, Message from Janette O'Neil, Chief Executive.

190 James D'Angelo, in Lorimer and Robinson, editors (2010) p. 207.

191 Hay (2007).

192 His Holiness the 14th Dalai Lama (2000) p. 192.

193 Muller (1982) quoted by King (2009) p. 106, and also see Ursula King (2010): "Earthing spiritual literacy: how to link spiritual development and education to a new Earth consciousness?" *Journal of Beliefs & Values: Studies in Religion and Education*, 31:3, 245–260, also online at http://www.tandfonline.com/doi/full/10.1080/13617672.2010.520998 sourced February 28, 2012.

194 www.globaljusticemovement.net/home/comparisons.htm sourced February 28, 2012.

195 For example King (2009) also Rudolf Steiner, Alastair McIntosh (2004), Lorimer and Robinson, editors (2010), H.H. the 14th Dalai Lama (2000).

196 From the Hindu faith statement written for Palmer with Finlay (2003) p. 96. Also at http://www.arcworld.org/faiths.asp?pageID=77 sourced February 28, 2012.

197 International Directory of Schools http://www.waldorf-schule.info/en/waldorfschule-bund/adresses/international-associations-and-waldorf-schools/index.html Association of Waldorf Schools of North America, AWSNA, http://www.whywaldorfworks.org/ sourced February 28, 2012. See also the wonderful film by Jonathan Stedall, *The Challenge of Rudolf Steiner*, http://jonathanstedall.co.uk/rudolf%20steiner.php/ sourced April 27, 2012.

198 McIntosh (2004) p. 117.

199 Lorimer and Robinson, editors (2010) pp. 211–12.

200 Skolimowski (2010).

201 See also for example the Revd V.A. Holmes-Gore MA, *Christ or Paul?* Renaissant Press, London, 1989 and "Jesus' Words Only" website for anyone interested in pursuing this line of thought further http://www.jesuswordsonly.com/ February 28, 2012.

202 See for example Dorr (2004) p. 29 *JSS*, drawing on ideas of Paulo Freire of 'generative themes' touching people's deep feelings to stir to action.

203 Wilber (2007) a book and method not without its critics.

204 Ratzinger (2005) pp. 143–144.

205 King, Ursula, "Can Spirituality Transform our World?" in *JSS*, Volume 1.1, 2011, p. 32.

206 *Phaedrus* by Plato http://ebooks.adelaide.edu.au/p/plato/p71phs/phaedrus.html sourced April 27, 2012.

207 Niebuhr (2009) p. xxvii.

208 Mehta (1987) p. 28.

209 For example the Scientific and Medical Network (SMN) is using crisis as the springboard for real practical and healing initiatives. Many SMN members have contributed their own ideas that have been brought together in Lorimer and Robinson, editors (2010). This could become a valuable resource for change. But while I am hopeful of such initiatives, I challenge the general sense displayed through many of those essays that religions as institutions were seen as damaging and a hindrance to the future well-being of the world; a view that I felt, then as now, to be devaluing the vital role religions can and do and indeed must play. See Stoneham "A New Renaissance: A Point of View," *Network Review*, Journal of the Scientific and Medical Network, Spring 2011 p. 12.

210 Mehta (1987) p. 307.

211 From *The Collected Works of C.G. Jung*, vol. 11 1969, p. 459 cited in Dunn (2000) p. 199.

Bibliography

Aristotle (1998) *Politics*, translated by Ernest Barker, revised R.F. Stalley, Oxford University Press, Oxford

Armstrong, Karen (2010) *The Case for God*, Vintage, London

Armstrong, Karen (2011) *Twelve Steps to a Compassionate Life*, The Bodley Head, London

Astley, J. (2002) *Ordinary Theology: Looking, Listening and Learning in Theology*, Ashgate, Aldershot

Bouquet, A.C. (1953) *Comparative Religion: A Short Outline*, Penguin, Harmondsworth

Campbell, Heidi (2005) *Exploring Religious Community Online. We Are One in the Network*, Routledge, London and New York

Clarke, Chris (2010) *Weaving the Cosmos: Science, Religion and Ecology*, O-Books, Hampshire

Dawkins, Richard (2006) *The God Delusion*, Bantam Press, London

Diamond, Jonathan (2002) *Narrative Means to Sober Ends: Treating Addiction and Its Aftermath*, Guilford Press, New York

Dorr, Donal (2004) *Time for a Change: A Fresh Look at Spirituality, Sexuality, Globalisation and the Church*, The Columba Press, Dublin

Dossey, Larry (2000) *Reinventing Medicine: Beyond Mind-Body to a New Era of Healing*, Element Books, Shaftesbury and Boston, Massachusetts; also a HarperCollins e-book; 1 edition July 24, 2007

Dossey, Larry (1989 and 1997) *Recovering the Soul: A Scientific and Spiritual Search*, Bantam Doubleday Dell Publishing Group, New York

Drane, John W. (2005) *Do Christians Know How to be Spiritual? The Rise of New Spirituality and the Mission of the Church*, Darton, Longman & Todd, London and Norwich

Du Bois, W.E.B. (2011) *The Souls of Black Folk*, www.create space.com

Dunn, Claire (2000) *Carl Jung: Wounded Healer of the Soul – An Illustrated Biography*, Continuum, London

Esposito, John L. and Mogahed, Dalia (2008) *Who Speaks For Islam: What a Billion Muslims Really Think*, Gallup Press, Washington

Flew, Antony (2007) *There is a God*, Harper One, New York

Foster, Charles (2010) *The Sacred Journey*, Thomas Nelson, Nashville

Gandhi, Mahatma (1958) *All Men Are Brothers: Life and Thoughts of Mahatma Gandhi as Told in His Own Words*, UNESCO, Paris

Gilbert, Paul (2010) *The Compassionate Mind*, Constable and Robinson, London

Grayling, A.C. (2004) *What is Good: The Search for the Best Way to Live*, Phoenix, Orion Books, London

H.H. the 14th Dalai Lama (2000) *Ancient Wisdom, Modern World: Ethics for the New Millennium*, Abacus, London

Hampton, Scott (2011) *Tolerant Oppression: Why promoting tolerance undermines our quest for equality and what we should do instead*, Dog Ear Publishing, Indianapolis

Hardy, Jean (2011) *A Wiser Politics: Psyche, Polis, Cosmos*, John Hunt Publishing, Hampshire

Harris, Sam (2005) *The End of Faith: Religion, Terror and the Future of Reason*, Simon and Schuster, London

Harvey, Andrew (2009) *The Hope: A Guide to Sacred Activism*, Hay House, London

Hay, David (2007) *Why Spirituality is Difficult for Westerners*, Societas, Exeter

Hick, John (2004) *An Interpretation of Religion: Human Responses to the Transcendent*, Palgrave Macmillan, Basingstoke and London

Holmes-Gore MA, The Revd V.A. (1989) *Christ or Paul?* Renaissant Press, London

Hunter, James Davison (2010) *To Change the World: The Irony, Tragedy and Possibility of Christianity in the Late Modern World*,

OUP, New York

Journal for the Study of Spirituality (JSS) Volume 1.1 (2011)

Jung, Carl (1970) *The Collected Works of C.G. Jung*, Princeton University Press

King, Ursula (2009) *The Search for Spirituality: Our Global Quest for Meaning and Fulfilment*, Canterbury Press, London

Koenig, Harold and McConnell, Malcolm (2001) *The Healing Power of Faith: How Belief and Prayer Can Help You Triumph Over Disease*, Simon & Schuster, NY

Koenig, Harold G. (2004) *The Healing Connection: The Story of a Physician's Search for the Link between Faith and Health*, Templeton Press, West Conshohocken, PA 19428 USA

Lennox, John C. (2007) *God's Undertaker: Has Science Buried God?* Lion Hudson, Oxford

Lennox, John C. (2011) *Gunning for God: Why the New Atheists are Missing the Target*, Lion Hudson, Oxford

Lorimer, David, and Robinson, Oliver, editors (2010) *A New Renaissance: Transforming Science, Spirit and Society*, Floris Books, Edinburgh

Lorimer, David (1990) *Whole in One: The Near-Death Experience and the Ethic of Interconnectedness*, Penguin Books, Harmondsworth

McGilchrist, Iain (2009) *The Master and His Emissary*, Yale University Press, New Haven and London

McGrath, Alister and McGrath, Joanna Collicutt (2007) *The Dawkins Delusion: Atheist Fundamentalism and the Denial of the Divine*, SPCK, London

McGrath, Alister (2005) *Dawkins' God: Genes, Memes and the Meaning of Life*, Blackwell, Oxford

McIntosh, Alastair (2004) *Soil and Soul: People versus Corporate Power*, Aurum Press, London

Medawar, Peter (new edition 1981) *Advice to a Young Scientist*, Basic Books, NY

Mehta, P.D. (1987) *The Heart of Religion*, Element Books, Shaftesbury, Dorset

Montefiore, Hugh (1997) *Time to Change: Challenge for an Endangered Planet*, The Bible Reading Fellowship, Abingdon UK

Morrison, Dylan (2011) *Prodigal Prophet*, www.createspace.com

Muller, Robert (1982) *New Genesis: Shaping a Global Spirituality*

Niebuhr, Gustav (2009) *Beyond Tolerance: How People Across America are Building Bridges Between Faiths*, Penguin Books, London

Niebuhr, Reinhold (1944) *The Children of Light and Children of Darkness: A Vindication of Democracy and a Critique of its Traditional Defense*, Charles Scribner's Sons, New York, also (2011) University of Chicago Press

Palmer, Martin with Finlay, Victoria (2003) *Faith in Conservation: New Approaches to Religions and the Environment*, The World Bank, Washington DC

Patel, Eboo (2007) *Acts of Faith: The Story of an American Muslim, the Struggle for the Soul of a Generation*, Beacon Press, Boston

Pattison, Stephen (2007) *The Challenge of Practical Theology*, Jessica Kingsley, London

Polkinghorne, John (1986) *One World: The Interaction of Science and Theology*, SPCK, London

Putnam, Robert D. and Campbell, David E. (2010) *American Grace: How Religion Divides and Unites Us*, Simon and Schuster, New York

Rankin, Aidan (2010) *Many-Sided Wisdom: A New Politics of the Spirit*, O-Books, Hampshire

Ratzinger, Cardinal Joseph (2005) *Truth and Tolerance – Christian Belief and World Religions*, Ignatius Press, San Francisco

Ray, Paul (2000) *The Cultural Creatives: How Fifty Million People are Changing the World*, Harmony

Sacks, Jonathan (2011) *The Great Partnership: God, Science and the Search for Meaning*, Hodder and Stoughton, London

Schluter, Michael and Ashcroft, John, editors (2005) *Jubilee Manifesto: A Framework, Agenda & Strategy for Christian Social*

Reform, Inter-Varsity Press, Illinois

Sheldrake, Rupert (2012) *The Science Delusion: Freeing the Spirit of Enquiry*, Hodder and Stoughton, London

Simpson, Anna, editor (2011) "Moving Mountains: How Can Faith Shape Our Future?" *Green Futures*

Skolimowski, Henryk (2010) *Let There be Light – the Mysterious Journey of Cosmic Creativity*, Wisdom Tree, New Delhi

Spencer, Nick and Alexander, Denis (2009) *Rescuing Darwin: God and Evolution in Britain Today*, Theos: London www.theos-thinktank.co.uk material and quotations used under Creative Commons Attribution-Noncommercial-No Derivative Works 2.5 license as extended with specific permission from Alanna Macleod for Theos email to author dated March 1, 2012

Stoneham, Eleanor (2011) *Healing This Wounded Earth: With Compassion, Spirit and the Power of Hope*, O-Books, Hampshire

Teilhard de Chardin, P. (1978) "The Great Monad," in *The Heart of Matter*, Collins, London

Tomlinson, Dave (2008) *Re-Enchanting Christianity: Faith in an Emerging Culture*, Canterbury Press, Norwich

USPG: Anglicans in World Mission, newspaper, *Transmission* (Spring 2012)

Volf, Miroslav, H.R.H. Prince Ghazi bin Muhammad of Jordan and Yarrington, Melissa, editors (2010) *A Common Word: Muslims and Christians on Loving God and Neighbor*, William B Eerdmans Publishing Company, Cambridge, UK

Wilber, Ken (2007) *Integral Spirituality: A Startling New Role for Religion in the Modern and Postmodern World*, Shambhala Publications, US

Williams, Peter S. (2009) *A Sceptic's Guide to Atheism*, Paternoster, Milton Keynes

Wilson, Andrew, editor (1991) *World Scripture: A Comparative Anthology of Sacred Texts*, Paragon House Publishers, New York

Circle Books

Circle is a symbol of infinity and unity. It's part of a growing list of imprints, including o-books.net and zero-books.net.

Circle Books aims to publish books in Christian spirituality that are fresh, accessible, and stimulating.

Our books are available in all good English language bookstores worldwide. If you can't find the book on the shelves, then ask your bookstore to order it for you, quoting the ISBN and title. Or, you can order online—all major online retail sites carry our titles.

To see our list of titles, please view www.Circle-Books.com, growing by 80 titles per year.

Authors can learn more about our proposal process by going to our website and clicking on Your Company > Submissions.

We define Christian spirituality as the relationship between the self and its sense of the transcendent or sacred, which issues in literary and artistic expression, community, social activism, and practices. A wide range of disciplines within the field of religious studies can be called upon, including history, narrative studies, philosophy, theology, sociology, and psychology. Interfaith in approach, Circle Books fosters creative dialogue with non-Christian traditions.

And tune into MySpiritRadio.com for our book review radio show, hosted by June-Elleni Laine, where you can listen to authors discussing their books.

MySpiritRadio